Luminos is the Open Access monograph publishing program from UC Press. Luminos provides a framework for preserving and reinvigorating monograph publishing for the future and increases the reach and visibility of important scholarly work. Titles published in the UC Press Luminos model are published with the same high standards for selection, peer review, production, and marketing as those in our traditional program. www.luminosoa.org

Things Unseen

Things Unseen

*Essays on Evidence, Knowledge,
and the Late Ancient World*

Ellen Muehlberger

UNIVERSITY OF CALIFORNIA PRESS

University of California Press
Oakland, California

© 2025 by Ellen Muehlberger

This work is licensed under a Creative Commons
CC BY license. To view a copy of the license,
visit http://creativecommons.org/licenses.

All other rights reserved.

Suggested citation: Muehlberger, E. *Things Unseen:
Essays on Evidence, Knowledge, and the Late Ancient
World*. Oakland: University of California Press, 2025.
DOI: https://doi.org/10.1525/luminos.253

Cataloging-in-Publication Data is on file at the Library of
Congress.

ISBN 978-0-520-42357-2 (cloth)
ISBN 978-0-520-42358-9 (pbk.)
ISBN 978-0-520-42359-6 (ebook)

GPSR Authorized Representative: Easy Access System Europe,
Mustamäe tee 50, 10621 Tallinn, Estonia,
gpsr.requests@easproject.com

34 33 32 31 30 29 28 27 26 25
10 9 8 7 6 5 4 3 2 1

For Dodds

CONTENTS

Preface ix

Introduction
1

1. Impossible Women
14

2. Foundations of Knowledge
53

3. The Advent of the Superfather
87

4. Faces in the Crowds
120

Acknowledgments 159

Bibliography 161

Index 177

PREFACE: NOT WHAT THEY SEEM

I picked up Henry Chadwick's *Early Christian Thought and the Classical Tradition* in 1997. I can still feel the sensation of pulling it from a row of books on the shelf, one finger hooked into the small valley between the covers, tipping the little book out top-end first from between its tightly packed neighbors and then wiggling it free. I was either in the used section of Schuler's on 28th Street in Grand Rapids, or in the old 84 Charing Cross store in Munising. I went to both in those years and I can only remember the shelf in front of me and the feeling of wanting that little book. The essays in it were a pleasurable hybrid of readable, yet authoritative, prose. To me, working as a fundraiser and just barely starting to think about applying to graduate school again, it was soothing. I liked reading it, just as I've liked reading other books like it— Simon Goldhill's *Foucault's Virginity*, Peter Brown's *The Making of Late Antiquity* and his *Power and Persuasion in Late Antiquity*, alongside others.

It was a while before I knew enough to understand exactly *why* I liked them. All those books came from invited lectures their authors had given on a theme and then revised, usually lightly, for print. The academic fields of ancient history, classics, and their adjacents like early Christian studies are brimming with such lecture series: the Stanford Memorial Lectures, the Curti Lectures, the Sather Lectures, even the Jerome Lectures here at the University of Michigan. The books that came from these opportunities share an easy, enticing tone. Because they started as lectures, they tend to be looser, freer, less directly tied to the things that show up in footnotes and bibliographies, more driven toward the desires of a live audience. There is less hedging in them and more asserting. They consistently aim to engage the reader with paradoxes presented and then solved, or long-held paradigms neatly upended and replaced. Reading them hinted at what it might be like to write them.

It was longer still before I recognized that books like these were the endpoint of a long process of selection. Invitations to give a lecture series are few and they are, as a rule, extended to the people with high standing in their field. That has meant senior scholars got invitations, while early career scholars—who are as likely to have three or four fascinating lectures in them—are just not asked. But "standing" in academia has to do with so much more than the length of one's career. It is also marked by the same predictable logic that gives more authority to men than to women, more credibility to white people than to anyone else. That logic is everywhere, but probably the easiest way to see what I am talking about is to Google the question, "what does a professor look like?" and view the image results. Add in just a smidge of academia's odd fixation on institutional prestige, and the economy of the lecture series invitation—who gets one, and when, and why—follows the same algorithm with the same results: senior, elite, white, and frequently bearded. And that is a shame, because the genre of the lecture series book is generative, summative, and field-changing. It is a genre that would benefit from a wider pool of participants; it also clearly benefits the writer. I wanted its license for myself, so I decided to fake it.

My first two books are evidenced within an inch of their lives. In them, I was deeply committed to proof, to notes, to comprehensive references. I learned a new language just to be able to cite six lines of a text that clinched an argument I wanted to make. That is, after all, what is expected in scholarly work: to make the effort and make it visible. The weight of the evidence I dragged into those books served me well; it was proof I could legitimately say what I was saying and, to be direct, the books fulfilled their professional purpose, each one earning me a promotion. But I call it "weight" intentionally—it was heavy work, and the habit of constant reference gradually made me hesitant to say *anything* without the same level of backup behind me, as if ancient texts could authorize me to think the ideas I have. That is another reason that this genre of writing appealed to me. It came with the challenge of simply claiming my thoughts as my own.

Reading other books helped me decide to just do it. Ali Smith's *Artful* was what originally got me thinking that I could fake a lecture series. By chance, I was reading it at the same time that I was reading Bram Stoker's second-best-known book, *Famous Impostors*, and the deal was sealed. My invitation had been issued. Here are four lectures I've never been asked to give, fronted with a short introduction to get us all on the same page.

Ann Arbor, December 31, 2024

Introduction

Without a Doubt

Near the turn of the second century, a follower of Jesus wrote a letter of explanation, correcting a common mistake. Jesus may have been executed, his crucifixion a spectacle perched by the Romans on a hilltop for all to see. But the ostensible message of that example—that he was pitiable, weak, or even criminal—was not in fact the truth. In truth, this follower argued, Jesus was far holier, his life far more significant, than people had really grasped. He was a son of God, and a favored son of God at that. How could other followers square the image of their leader's broken corpse planted atop the hill with the claim that Jesus was divine? And perhaps more challenging, how could they hold on to their conviction when the majority of the world around them did not see it? The *Letter to the Hebrews* explained that anyone who did not understand Jesus the same way that his followers did simply lacked faith, which the author then helpfully defined: "Faith," he wrote, "is the assurance of things hoped for, the conviction of things not seen."[1]

1. Hebrews 11:1.

Faith is a possession, and if it is held, it brings a sense of confidence, even security, in one's perspective. It allowed knowledge about Jesus that was hard to come by in other ways.

Ironically, the readers of the *Letter to the Hebrews* were not expected to take this assertion about faith on faith. Instead, the author pointed out examples, men in the community's past whose lives demonstrated the guarantee he was trying to persuade them of. There were men of old who had acted in the face of prevailing headwinds, when both apparent reality and common sense dictated that they should do something else. Noah, for example, inhabited a world of sunshine and fair winds when he received a warning from God that only he could hear. Acting "by faith" and according to that warning, he built an ark for the coming storm rather than trusting what he could see. Then Abraham, a father to a miraculous child, prepared to do the unthinkable, standing ready to slaughter the child he had expected for so long and thus to end his legacy, solely on God's request. Moses, too, early in life chose to be among his own people, when there was an obviously easier path of staying with the Egyptian pharaoh and becoming his adopted son. These exemplary men and others like them acted contrary to all indications. They moved against common knowledge, with only faith to provide the surety they needed in order to act. It was their guarantee, and in turn, these men of old became a guarantee to others. In the *Letter* they are described as "a cloud of witnesses," there to testify to what everyone else should already know. By trusting in God and not what they could sense themselves, these men all did right. Or, as the author of *Hebrews* says, "by faith, our ancestors received approval."[2]

---

2. Hebrews 11:2.

At the time of its composition in the second century, the *Letter to the Hebrews* was an exhortation to a minority. The followers of Jesus were few, and they were scattered. The author of this letter did not know that his words would one day form part of the canonical collection Christians call the New Testament; he did not even use the word "Christian" or "Christianity" in the *Letter*. When he wrote, he had real doubt that others in the world would ever come to understand Jesus's life and purpose as he had. Indeed, he worried that others like him would give up on their shared understanding—that is why he wrote the *Letter* in the first place, to shore them up.[3] In his world, the majority followed what evidence was available, and it seemed to say that Jesus had been executed as a criminal—a squashed threat to the state—and his followers rightfully dispersed and dispossessed. The minority, for its part, needed to hold on to what it knew, even in the face of what it saw, lest all hope be lost.

There was no way for the author of the *Letter to the Hebrews* to know that his perspective on Jesus's life would come to be the foundation of a tradition that influenced everything from imperial politics and public architecture to law and juridical power, education, domestic relations, and economics. He had no sense of how deeply it would pervade the entirety of the world that he knew, and that it would extend further still, out beyond the limits of his geographical imagination. As the centuries passed, an increasing number of people came to have the understanding that the *Letter to the Hebrews* advocated. Slowly, in small numbers at first, then suddenly, everywhere, there were followers of

3. On how to understand the perspective of Hebrews and other first- and second-century texts that are later claimed as part of Christian tradition, see Maia Kotrosits, *Rethinking Early Christian Identity: Affect, Violence, and Belonging* (Fortress, 2015).

Jesus—Christians—who saw his life just as the author of the *Letter* had hoped they would. This was such a stark change in culture that it even changed how the *Letter* itself was read. Looking back from later centuries, readers saw it as a Christian text, offering to the Christian movement an early witness to lofty interpretations of Jesus's nature as Christ. Authors write to their own situations, but texts naturally live on. Occasional in its own time, the *Letter to the Hebrews* became foundational when encountered centuries later in late antiquity.

In this new context, the *Letter*'s pronouncements about faith surely landed differently. There are not many direct commentaries on the *Letter* that survive from late antiquity, but as Christianity grew, important texts were translated into new languages for new audiences. Translations are a valuable record of a text's reception, because they capture in their variations the translator's attempt to make the meaning of a text clear: The choices a translator makes, the exposition she adds, can point to interpretations peculiar to her or her community. The late ancient Syriac translation of the *Letter to the Hebrews* gives the *Letter*'s promise about faith more heft by adding to its definition. To translate the verse that we have seen as "Faith is the assurance of things hoped for, the conviction of things not seen," the Syriac offers

> Faith is the assurance of hopeful things, as if they were extant in reality, and the revelation of things not seen.
>
> 'ytyh dyn hymnwt' pys' 'l 'ylyn d'ytyhyn bsbr' 'yk hw dhwy lhyn bsw'rn '. wglyn' d'ylyn dl' mtḥzyn.

Here, a late ancient writer makes explicit what had previously been implicit: By the time this translation was created in the fourth or maybe the early fifth century, the faith that the *Letter* describes included an unseen reality that Christians could grasp with that faith.

Late ancient translations of the *Letter* also disclose new meaning imparted to the verse that comes next, the one about the "approval" given to the ancients. Two different versions—one Latin, one Syriac—agree about what the verse meant. Instead of "approval" given to the ancients, they both see something more substantive where faith is.

> Latin: By this faith, the ancients arrived at evidence.
> *in hac enim testimonium consecuti sunt senes*
>
> Syriac: In this faith was evidence for the ancients.
> *wbhd' hwt shdwt' 'l qshysh'*

Composed at roughly the same time, but by two different translators, working in two different languages, these renderings converge on a single idea: faith made a path to evidence. Here we notice that late ancient readers saw in the *Letter to the Hebrews* a promise. The faith it described meant there was, and always had been, proof available to the faithful, evidence to be relied on where none could easily be found, a testimony to things others could not sense and did not know.

I begin with this famous passage from the *Letter to the Hebrews* and its readings by later Christians because they bring to light a pattern of knowing that persists in Christianity. Already in the *Letter* itself, the writer posits two groups of people—namely, those who already understand what Jesus was and what his life signified, and those who do not. The later translators saw that duality, surely, but what they added in expansion suggests they also saw a twoness to reality: what could be apprehended without faith and then the additional reality available to those with who had faith. With the two existing in parallel, there is always the tension of the matter not quite resolved, the duality waiting to be reduced to a unity. To make things even more complex, there comes ported within this concept of faith also two eras: one in which faith's evidence is not yet known to all, and one when it finally will be. Put another way, Christian knowledge is at its core apocalyptic—meaning, in Christianity the pattern of duality and its resolution, of waiting for the delayed but inevitable revelation of knowledge appears over and over again, almost fractally, present at scales both grand and small.

Now, in modern usage, *apocalyptic* usually refers to terrible things, like dissolution or catastrophe. Technically, that is incorrect—word mavens will tell you that apocalypse simply means the revealing of something previously hidden. It is etymologically analogous to the word *discovery*, with no value judgement imparted at all. Regardless of how often people try to correct this usage, the distinctive sense of destruction sticks to the word. So, it can be very hard for us to recognize just how *constructive* the apocalyptic bent of knowledge in Christianity could be. The horizon of promised revelation, the resolution of the always-present duality, these are structures that store potential energy; the Christian shape of knowledge is a bit like an engine running on idle, ready to produce power once it is engaged.

After the legitimization of Christianity in the early fourth century, the visible presence of Christians grew, with new buildings and monuments arising in the landscape; public rituals, cult celebrations, and pilgrimage sites multiplying in public life; inscriptions and dedications appearing in ever new places; and an explosion of literary activity across various genres, from the historical and exhortatory to the hagiographical and epistolary. Viewed one way, all these visible markers of Christian culture are expressions of the tradition's increasing dominance in late antiquity—both modern scholars and ancient Christians interpreted these forms as proof of the Christianization of the Roman Empire and eventually the wider Mediterranean. Of course, that is true. Public culture can be at once a legible deposit of power and also the means through which to naturalize that power. At the same time, we should understand that the inclination to apocalyptic patterns of knowing drove this remarkable production of culture. The impulse to make so much is about having something to show for faith—the thing hoped for that could be seen when it was eventually built, written, or performed.

This project joins a very lively collection of studies on the topic of knowledge in the late ancient world. That term, *knowledge*, is meant to signal that what is under study is not solely the *content* of what late ancient people knew but the processes and structures that enabled, created, and transmitted that content. The particular benefit of *knowledge* as an analytical term is to surpass the simple idea that ancient people knew different things than we do (and by implication, knew wrong things compared to our right things). Instead, ancient people *knew* differently; they processed and evaluated and transmitted knowledge, sustained the entire framework of knowledge, differently. This approach to knowledge also allows for a different accounting of relative *progress*. The people we study were not just earlier on our path toward science or secularization but lived in a different world with a unique array of possible futures ahead of them, only one of which happens to be the one we now inhabit. That is probably why the notion of exploring knowledge has been as popular as it is in the field of religious studies; for one, it allows for talking about worldviews that include what we might in passing call the supernatural without having to discuss them *as* supernatural, or to accept them (or implicitly accept them) as fact.

With respect to antiquity, different projects in the study of knowledge have focused on different aspects of how knowledge was created and maintained. For example, in the volume *Late Ancient Knowing*, Mike Chin and Moulie Vidas collected essays that explored common concepts—God, the cosmos, medicine, the emperor—and investigated how these things were known by ancient people. The emphasis of the volume landed on the way the world was imagined to be and how it was assumed to work.[4] There are other avenues of inquiry. Tim Whitmarsh and Jason König, in their volume *Ordering Knowledge in the Roman Empire*, considered the effect of the empire's power relations on fields like literature, medicine, and architecture. As they argued, the process of knowing "cannot be divorced from particular social relations and situations. It is not some abstract activity, practiced from a position of detachment; rather it is enacted within all institutions of social encounter."[5] This is a crucial insight. The kind of knowledge that informs fields as disparate as cosmology, or theories of the body, or standards of measurement all proceed from mechanisms that have their iterations at the level of the person.

The person is also inevitably taken as another object to be known. Late ancient Christians created entire catalogs of knowledge about groups of people they considered error-bound. There were the Christians who did not adhere to the correct creed or festal schedule; those who performed the wrong rituals, or at least not the right ones; other Christians who collaborated too closely with, or not closely enough with, Roman power; there were groups of old, like Hellenists, Stoics, Jews, barbarians, or new

---

4. C. M. Chin and Moulie Vidas, eds., *Late Ancient Knowing: Explorations in Intellectual History* (University of California Press, 2015).

5. Jason König and Tim Whitmarsh, eds., *Ordering Knowledge in the Roman Empire*, (Cambridge University Press, 2007), 6.

groups like the Ishmaelites; and still others who lived too close to some unseen line demarcating "Christian" from everyone else. Christian writers categorized all these types in treatises on heresy, where the faults of real and imaginary groups were laid out in encyclopedic detail. The practice of writing this literature is, as Todd Berzon has argued, aligned with the genre of ancient ethnography, the literature that identified and described non-Roman peoples by assigning them characteristics according to group and by drawing boundaries to mark "them" apart from the ethnographer's "us."[6]

So, heresiology as a discipline takes as its object those who seem proximate and describes them as distant. It is a well-defined genre of late ancient Christian writing, and at the same time, it is salient in modern narratives about early Christianity and its efforts at boundary-making, marked as such in handbooks of early Christian studies. Yet heresiology does not contain all there is to be investigated—what else there is may require a different method of looking. It is especially important to try because, as Annette Yoshiko Reed has observed, Christianity's patterns of knowing have long shaped other realms of knowledge, including the field of religious studies and the very concept of religion itself.[7] Reed's observation bears out in the study of early Christianity, as concepts, chronologies, and categories established by the tradition can still determine how scholars and students approach it now. The more parts of the machine of Christian knowledge-making

---

6. Todd Berzon, *Classifying Christians: Ethnography, Heresy, and the Limits of Knowledge in Late Antiquity* (University of California Press, 2016).

7. Annette Yoshiko Reed, "Method, Ethics, and Historiography: Tracing a Global Late Antiquity from and beyond Christianity," *Ancient Jew Review*, January 26, 2022.

that are diagrammed, the better—both the large structures and the smaller cogs.

What follows are four examinations of the small cogs. Mostly, I consider how Christians know about others: how they come by the confidence, then the evidence, that they already know the nature or capacities of other people. The first essay, "Impossible Women," traces the influence of a practice writing exercise on the way that men knew women in late antiquity. Practicing speaking as a woman was an exercise that all the ancient writers whose work we know did as boys, and that practice along the way gave them an experience that stood as evidence: they knew, and could speak for, the women they encountered in their adult lives. As we will see, Christian writers practiced speechmaking for women, and this peculiar way of thinking about others found its way into Christian hagiography. The second essay, "Foundations of Knowledge," watches as late ancient Christians go looking for evidence of deviance. Realizing that external signs of Christianness, like baptism or church attendance, were slight guarantee, Christians with suspicions of others found proof about problematic people in an odd place: the contents of their houses. Drawing from scholarship that has identified the relationship in the late ancient imagination between people and their dwellings, this essay reveals how intimately entangled Christian authority was with property.

The third chapter, "The Advent of the Superfather," tells the origin story of a new category of human being that emerged in the sixth century, something that Christian tradition itself did not name but that nonetheless forever changed the nature of authorship in the tradition. Cyril of Alexandria died in the fifth century, but after his death, he moved into a new station, beyond just that of a revered "father of the church." The actions taken at the Second Council of Constantinople have habitually been considered evidence of human frailty, but I argue that the council simply registered Cyril's emergence as a superfather, who, like a superhero, had altered reality wherever he appeared, bending previously immutable laws. All three of these essays point to the lasting influence of knowledge structures from the ancient world on our way of thinking. Then, the fourth essay, "Faces in the Crowds," turns explicitly toward the modern world, to examine our responses to the so-called Fayyum portraits, the mesmerizing and much-admired paintings of ancient faces. They appear to be evidence of individual lives from late antiquity—a very hard thing to come by, and thus very valuable. The senses of mystery and intimacy they evoke, however, are illusory effects. They are not ancient portraits, but modern objects created in the nineteenth century by the selective harvest of portions of funerary objects and designed to appeal to viewers already trained by modern technology to see individuality, essence, and truth in faces.

The choices I have made in these topics may seem idiosyncratic. What do imaginary women, the insufficiently converted, a theological prodigy, and the modern collecting of ancient objects have to do with the problem of evidence? And, moreover, what do they have to do with each other? Before I answer, let me say: this is the beauty of the lecture series. As a genre, it is often a grab bag, chronologically and topically adventurous, a kind of writing that asks you to trust the expert hand that created it, even before you begin to listen. In truth, lectures are a kind of magic show.

What do I hope to make you see in this one? First of all, I want to show you that late ancient Christianity is a rich field for investigation. That is true even for, or especially for, questions that late ancient Christians may not have themselves entertained. There are definitely processes at work under the surface, dynamic and consequential in ancient culture but surely still humming along in our own. Some readers will see the thread of patriarchy that runs through the book, which informs the access to education, the authority, the personhood that Christian men and not women were granted (and, if I am honest, inspired the writing of this book in the first place). Others will recognize that knowledge, in the processes I examine in this book, always comes borne on a tide of affect—whether it is the pleasure, the thrill even, of revealing something hidden about someone else that you alone can access, the doubt or anger that prompts interrogation of someone who does not seem quite right, the perplexity that arrives when people do not act as we think they should, or the wonder that arises at the prospect of being able to touch, even in the imagination, an individual who lived so long ago. Still others may see things I do not say here. If you are driven to search out a theme you see by either paging back through this book to thread it together or starting your own inquiry, then I daresay the magic has worked on you, too.

At the same time, though, I firmly believe we should always hold our sense of coherence up for question. What belongs or doesn't, what can illumine what—these are evaluations based on esteem and tradition. The tradition of Christianity has, of course, its own ideas about what counted as a significant development or an important text from its classical age, but we do not have to limit our inquiries to those ideas. Sometimes, we can introduce new specimens alongside well-studied species, put a seemingly esoteric text next to a canonical one, or place a man received as a titan of the past in conversation with his contemporaries to see how he fares. Alternately, we can break with categories altogether and jumble the evidence, genre against genre, medium against medium, type against type. At base, if something was created or read or used *in* late antiquity, it can be evidence for us *of* late antiquity, regardless of whether subsequent traditions value it or even recognize it. New knowledge of the old can be found in the seemingly "small," the "peripheral," because none of these things are small or peripheral for the people who made them and kept them. The trick, more often than not, is to reveal *why* they are thought small or peripheral, how they have come to be judged that way and until now left as things unseen.

CHAPTER ONE

Impossible Women

How Boys Learned to Know

Let me tell you a story about how knowledge is made.

It is an afternoon in the fourth century, and a boy of fourteen has come to join his teacher's circle of students in, let's say, Antioch. The teacher, well-known and revered by his students, has given the boy a kind of writing assignment. The boy will work on it for several sessions, composing something, performing it aloud, getting feedback from the teacher and maybe from other boys, revising it, then performing it aloud again. The boy is not alone in being assigned the task, and what he has been given to do is not unique. It is something that boys across the Mediterranean are doing and that boys who have studied with his teacher have long done. It is a strange task, but he starts on it—there are emperors and bishops among the teacher's former students, after all, so clearly something about his curriculum is working.[1] That kind of

---

1. For an example of the long reach of this classroom experience, see Susanna Elm, *Sons of Hellenism, Fathers of the Church: Emperor Julian, Gregory of Nazianzus, and the Vision of Rome*, Transformation of the Classical Heritage 49 (University of California Press, 2012).

storied future might wait for the boy on the horizon, but between him and it lie a thousand lessons, a thousand practice sessions, the first of which is to complete today's work: to compose a speech that answers the question *tinas an eipoi logous pornē sōphronēsasa*, or "What would a prostitute who has come to her senses say?"[2]

It is not an open prompt, where the boy can just write whatever comes to mind. Instead, it is a narrower invitation, to create an answer in the format known as "speech in character," a genre of imaginary writing that was a staple of rhetorical education in antiquity. Students were given questions that specified a character and a situation—like the prostitute who comes to her senses, among many others—and then asked to compose a speech in first-person voice that would capture the character's reaction and prospects. Some other prompts that survive from ancient classrooms ask students to step into the personae of famous characters already known to them from mythology: like "What would Achilles say as the Greeks are losing?" or "What would Cain say, having killed Abel and carrying his corpse?" But the prompt assigned to our boy on this afternoon belongs to a different subtype, one that required him to write something more abstract. It asked him not about a specific person from a classical story but about a generic character without name or distinct individuality—in other words, a type.

The two kinds of exercise in speech in character, one for famous characters and one for types, relied on different techniques to make them interesting. The speeches that teachers assigned for famous characters tended to catch them at pitched moments in the plot, like in the examples above just before a battle was about to

2. Libanius, *Progymnasmata* 11.18.1, in *Libanii Opera*, vol. 8, *Progymnasmata*, ed. R. Foerster (Tuebner, 1915), 414–15.

be lost or just after a murder had been committed. Drawing from the drama of commonly known stories, they focused on reversals of fortune to create conflict and thus tension in the speech. But the exercises that asked boys to speak as a type—as a prostitute, a eunuch, a farmer, a painter, and so on—these had to find their charge somehow else, and they did it by placing the typed character in a scenario that stood opposed to the very thing that defined them. Exactly because of who they were, these types found themselves ill-equipped to handle their circumstances.

So, for example, a student could be tasked with conjuring a speech in response to this question: *tinas an eipoi logous eunouchos erōn*, or "What would a eunuch say upon falling in love?"[3] The implied tension lies between the subject's body and what he wants; a eunuch—that is, a castrated man—could not possibly participate in love.[4] To be direct, the assumption is that penetrative sex is necessary to fulfill *erōs*, and so love would be out of this man's reach. You might ask, "Surely a man could find love without that kind of sex, or any sex at all?" In the asking, you have revealed one of the most valuable things about these speeches as historical sources: though they are by definition imaginary and by design impossible, they work by putting two commonly held ancient norms opposite one another, and thus show us by exception what the rules actually are.

In the question our boy was asked to consider, the implicit assumption is that a prostitute could not possibly come to her

---

3. Libanius, *Progymnasmata* 11.26.1.
4. Antonio Stramaglia, "Amori impossibili: P.Köln 250, le raccolte proginnasmatiche e la tradizione retorica dell' 'amante di un ritratto,'" in *Studium Declamatorium: Untersuchungen zu Schulübungen und Prunkreden von der Antike bis zur Neuzeit*, ed. Bianca-Jeanette Schröder and Jens-Peter Schröder, Beiträge zur Altertumskunde 176 (Sauer, 2003).

senses, meaning that she as a type was not capable of the quality the prompting question has asked him to attach to her—namely, *sōphrosynē*. This quality is difficult to pin down in translation—in the question, I have rendered "having acquired *sōphrosynē*" as "coming to one's senses." But all its potential meanings are positive: it could mean *wisdom, prudence, agency, moderation,* or *self-determination*. As a quality, it consistently gets praise in ancient philosophical classrooms and texts, in ascetic contexts, in friendship letters, and in exhortative treatises. There, it is what the best of men say that other men should be. Whether it is even possible for women is an open question.

But it is certainly not possible for the *pornē*, the woman for whom the boy is to speak. *That* word in Greek is a singular adjective, which can stand by itself to indicate a person who performs *porneia*, a word most often translated as fornication. In most contexts, translators render pornē as prostitute, as I have here.[5] Yet that is a shorthand, and it does not encompass all the possibilities. According to the usage of the fourth century, a pornē could be a woman who performs sex work, but it could also be a woman who has committed adultery. It could be used for a woman who marries again after assuming that her long-missing husband has in fact died. Or it could be a woman who behaved lewdly, a woman who stopped adhering to a religious discipline, a woman

---

5. Though what the *pornē* performs need not be a sexual act. Aline Roussell defines it as the "manifestation of desire for another's body." See Aline Roussell, *Porneia: On Desire and the Body in Antiquity*, trans. Felicia Pheasant (Basil Blackwell, 1988), 4. The word in the student's prompt, *pornē*, as a feminine adjective, is a shorthand for what we today would call a sex worker. The student writing the exercise would certainly call her a prostitute, or some other term that bore with it sexual shame, as that forms the tension with her other quality, *sōphrosynē*. For more on representations of women in sex work in the ancient world, see Jo Dowlingsoka, "Refiguring Sex Work in the Life of Theodoros of Sykeon," *SLA* 6 (2022): 457–81.

who put on makeup or jewelry, or a woman who in some unspecified way has "opposed God."[6] I have done more than one of these things; most people reading this have, too; I am doing at least one as I write this. We could make things simpler by saying just that a *pornē* was a woman not living according to cultural norms for what is decent or respectable.

The possibility that any woman could have both qualities—being a *pornē* and also having developed *sōphrosynē*—would have been a paradox, their incoherence making the assigned speech rather difficult to write. To make the challenge even steeper, our boy probably does not know much about wisdom or self-determination as of yet; he likely knows even less of women, especially fornicating women. Yet he was asked for this exercise to speak as if he were an expert in both. Of course, the word *expert* is derived from *experience*, of which our boy has precious little. The goal of this person making a realistic speech for a character who cannot be real is absurd—so absurd that the impossibility usually becomes part of the speech; ancient model answers to these prompts often have the speaking character themselves remark on how incredible or unbelievable their own story turns out to be.

So, honestly, why do it? Why assign a boy such a strange composition exercise? I have to ask because ancient educators made boys speak as female characters remarkably frequently. Of the extant examples of speeches in character composed in antiquity, about a third of them ask students to act as if they were women.[7]

---

6. G. W. H. Lampe and Henry George Liddell, eds., *A Patristic Greek Lexicon* (Clarendon, 1961), 1121–22. I make this argument despite the signs that in some earlier Greek literature, *sōphrosynē* could be a feminine virtue. See Christopher Moore, *The Virtue of Agency: Sôphrosunê and Self-Constitution in Classical Greece* (Oxford University Press, 2023).

7. Martin Kraus, "Rehearsing the Other Sex: Impersonation of Women in Ancient Classroom Ethopoeia," in *Escuela y Leteratura en Grecia*, ed. José

Educators continued to ask it of boys long after late antiquity. As Marjorie Curry Woods has observed, "schoolboy performances of speeches in the voices of emotional female characters are one of the most consistent, or at least recurring, aspects of pedagogy in the long history of all-male learning environments in the European West."[8] But to pretend to be a woman, any kind of woman, does not prepare one for oratory, or legal argument, or historical narration—that is, the ostensible learning goals of the rhetorical classroom. Practicing a woman's voice for these genres would be no help for those future endeavors, and could even be a harm, as orators who acted or sounded "womanly" were roundly criticized.[9] Some speculate that the practice of "temporarily inhabiting the emotions of another gender" gave boys a release valve, and could have even been fun.[10] But, if boys so entertained were to act this way at any other time in their lives without the framework of an exercise, they would court the charge, ironically, of acting like women. So, a boy writes in a voice that cannot be, for a scenario that does not exist, without any relevant experience of the conditions that structure the exercise, and for no discernible future gain. What purpose could this work possibly serve? Why spend time practicing something that you can never do again? Speeches of women were prevalent enough, though, that these boys were certainly accomplishing *something*.

Antonio Fernández Delgado et al. (Edizioni dell'Università degli Studi di Cassino, 2007), 457.

8. Marjorie Curry Woods, *Weeping for Dido: The Classics in the Medieval Classroom* (Princeton University Press, 2019), chapter 3, "Boys Performing Women (and Men): The Classics and After," 137.

9. Kraus, "Rehearsing the Other Sex," 456–59. On the disparagement of womanly orators, see Kate Wilkinson, *Women and Modesty in Late Antiquity* (Cambridge University Press, 2015), esp. 90–94.

10. Woods, *Weeping for Dido*, 146.

Speaking as another person under these circumstances was, I argue, practice for being powerful. It taught you that your imagination, however shallow or inexperienced (we *are* talking about fourteen-year-olds here), was enough to provide you with knowledge of someone else, their motivations, and certainty about the right actions for them to take. That is to say, composing speeches like these taught self-assurance, conveyed feelings of confidence through the enactment of confident performance of the supposedly unfamiliar, and even created a sense of mastery in young boys like ours. It was not just a matter of their sense of themselves, but their sense of others. But there is more. These imagined exercises created examples of impossible women, who then persisted in the imagination, parallel to reality. I will argue that they came to stand in place of the kind of empirical knowledge one could gain by meeting, interacting with, and even living with, actual women. Speeches in character, even though they were deliberately made up—indeed, *especially* because they were made up—worked to instill a disposition of arrogance and a confident, self-generated knowledge of others that were unshakeable in the face of constant, iterated, real-world contact with those others.[11] As he composes, the boy's work shapes his mind and ultimately his world so that he thinks he knows others better than they know themselves.

I: ANTIQUITY'S TOP MODELS

How can a little exercise—an absurd made-up speech—do all that? Let me show you.

11. The fictitiousness of the speeches is crucial. There is something about playing at being someone that is perversely more effective at making power than just being told, "You're more powerful than them."

The classroom where the boy would practice was an intimate space, where students spent their days learning by memorizing, imitating, performing, and being closely evaluated by their teacher. It was, on the one hand, a place of ease. Tutoring in the art of rhetoric cost enough money that most of the students came from elite families, and they usually were all boys who had been raised with the expectation that the same wealth and power and networks their fathers enjoyed would be theirs. Yet the classroom was also a place of terror. Learning was corporal, and teachers beat boys regularly for a host of reasons; the violence among students themselves could also be quite harsh. Under these circumstances, peculiar cultures formed, specific to the group but, to its participants, seemingly universal—the lessons, the beatings, the competition, and the ways of thought they all engendered came to seem to be simply the way things were. The culture shaped by rhetorical practice was the foundation of how elite men thought about and knew the world; the reality that they all agreed to and trained themselves on in these classrooms carried forward. Boys here learned how to approach the world, how to imagine it, and importantly, how to expect the world to meet them when they ventured out to see it.

To see the peculiar culture formed by rhetorical education, we have two kinds of evidence. The first, far more abundant, are the results of this curriculum: the careers, orientations, and ethics of the men trained this way, as we can find it in their surviving writing. The rebar of rhetorical training is visible in the shape of their intellectual creations.[12] The second kind of evidence, harder to come by, is seen in the tools of the classroom, where they survive.

---

12. Ellen Muehlberger, *Moment of Reckoning: Imagined Death and Its Consequences in Late Ancient Christianity* (Oxford University Press, 2019), esp. "Training for Death," 105–45.

For prompts like this boy's exercise, we have several dozen full responses, some perhaps created by students, but most composed by teachers, as models for the students to imitate when they had to compose their own.[13] For the question about the wise prostitute specifically, the famous rhetorical teacher Libanius of Antioch composed a model that survives, and it is as linguistically complex as you would expect a rhetorician's model to be. We are going to look at the grammatical details of his response, because its complexity comprises both a preening virtuosity of language and a theory of what a woman might be.

Embedded in the model's words for the speaker is a commentary about her newfound agency. The prompt, you'll remember, tells us that something has happened: a fornicating woman who, by definition, cannot embody sōphrosynē, suddenly has gained it. As we listen to her speech, we are brought to realize that she comes online as a self-possessed agent only slowly. Libanius encodes this in his grammatical choices for her speech. The first two sentences of the model response establish a baseline. She says:

> Let pimps be gone from me! I am not to be sold to any comer for two or three coins. Let someone destroy for me the dedications of my lovers—whose pollutions I reject even the mere memory of—in the sanctuary of Aphrodite from the lovers of the Cyprian![14]

At first glance, these words highlight her new confidence: She is telling others what to do. At the same time, the speaker commands

---

13. Eugenio Amato and Gianluca Ventrella, "L'éthopée dans la pratique scolaire et littéraire," in 'ΗΘΟΠΟΙΙΑ: *La représentation de caractères à l'époque impériale et tardive*, ed. Eugenio Amato and Jacques Schamp (Helios, 2005).

14. Libanius, *Progymnasmata* 11.18.1: "Ἐρρέτω μοι γένος προαγωγῶν. οὐκέτι δύο καὶ τριῶν ὀβολῶν τῷ προσιόντι πιπράσκομαι. καθελεῖ μοί τις τὰ περὶ τὴν Κύπριν τῶν ἐραστῶν ἀναθήματα, ὧν καὶ τῇ μνήμῃ μόνῃ μέμφομαι τὰ μιάσματα."

something—"Let pimps be gone from me!" and "Let someone destroy for me!"—but she only appears as the indirect object of these commands, the person for whom or to whom someone else is meant to act. In terms of the available formats in ancient Greek, she barely appears amidst the commands, discernible only in the short little particle *moi*. Then, each of those commands is followed by a clause in which the speaker does indeed use a verb about herself: "I am not to be sold," and "I reject." Yet those verbs appear in forms in Greek that are different from the active form. That is to say, they take an active meaning, but they do not *look* like something active.[15]

Libanius just happened to choose these two verbs, but not by accident. I say "just happened to," but Libanius is a deliberate writer creating a model to be preserved and transmitted and imitated; if he was ever conscious of his choice of words, it is in models like these. Although the meaning of both verbs is active, it is unmistakable that Libanius here has made form his subtle messenger, doubly so because he has done it twice in a row. When this character begins to speak, she is issuing commands, but she only appears in oblique cases relative to those commands—grammatically, they are things that happen *to* her. Nevertheless, as those commands set in motion her renunciation of a system of external control, she begins to emerge as an agent, though at first an agent whose influence just for now is limited, signaled by the use of these verb forms.

These are, of course, a rhetorician's tricks. Libanius is showing off, trying to make the reader say, "I see what you did there, yes, how clever. What command you have of the language!" Displays of skill, though, are never without meaning. As the speech

---

15. In order, the first is passive, the second deponent.

continues, Libanius uses his craft to signal, again, the woman's strange new agency. The speaker, who once existed without sōphrosynē, had no self-possession, no perspective on her actions. Once the conditions of the prompt were established, though, once the switch has been flipped, so to speak, she possesses wisdom so fully that she now takes its perspective to all the phases of her life: present, past, and future.

We can see this in the next part of the model speech, where, in the space of about forty words, Libanius chooses the same form of the verb *nine times*:

> I used to pluck the rose; I used to train in shamelessness; I used to dream of even worse; I used to work hard to make the nighttime even more shameful than the day; still entangled [with one man] I used to hunt the guy nearby; I used to joke, gossiping under my breath to a neighbor. I used to possess the robber; I used to love the disowned one; I used to have a house full of inappropriate men.[16]

This purposeful repetition of the same verb form is, on one level, merely a demonstration of his skill. But it also reveals the new character of the speaker to us: She had of course lived through the events in her own past when they happened, had done the deeds to do the deed, but according to late ancient assumptions about women like her, she had not had at that point the voice to speak about any of it as her own, to name what was happening as her own plans. Now, though, once the switch of sōphrosynē has been thrown, she has words about her past—words for naming, words for confessing, words for realizing. Her voice is loosed, and the

16. Libanius, Progymnasmata 11.18.2: "ἥρπαζον τὸ ῥόδον, ἤσκουν τὴν ἀναισχυντίαν, ὠνειροπόλουν τὰ χείρονα, ἔσπευδον τὴν νύκτα τῆς ἡμέρας αἰσχροτέραν ἐργάσασθαι. ἔτι περιπλεκομένη τὸν δεῖνα τὸν πλησίον ἐθήρευον, ἐπέσκωπτον τῷ γείτονι ψιθυρίζουσα. ἐμὸς ἦν ὁ λῃστής, ἐφίλουν τὸν ἀποκήρυκτον, μεστὴν εἶχον τὴν οἰκίαν ἀνδρῶν ἀπρεπῶν."

claims to agency—"I used to do this, I used to do that," with herself as the subject—come pouring out of her, rapid fire.

Like I explained above, none of this is really even possible according to the norms shared among students about what women are like in general and what fornicating women are like in particular. Women who fornicate are not self-possessed, so they do not act according to reason or even a measured will.[17] Yet, the verbal magic of this exercise has turned her into an agent, not solely for the moment when she realizes it, but retroactively throughout the life she had led while not (yet) wise. On the one hand, Libanius enacts her agency slowly, unfurling it in the technicalities of the Greek he uses in the model; on the other hand, the character says words she could only say if she has already always been wise. The two together create an otherworldly effect: the transformation that has made her wise could not have taken place in her experience—it has happened, she speaks of it as if it and she were real, and we are now seeing what such a woman would say if she could only have seen it. She looks real, but she inhabits a perspective that she could never have come to have if she were actually the thing she is typed to be. A kind of two-tier person is created: real and unreal, impossible and possible.

Which is to say that she only appears real because of Libanius's skill at imagining her. It is his power on display in this model speech, not hers. He creates entire worlds with his words, worlds where the rules do not apply, and she exists there, as his playground, the field on which his ideas about the pornē and sōphrosynē are all worked out. So, through his words in her

---

17. In contrast to the types of speech in character that depend on lament and regret—namely, those based on well-known characters from stories—this woman recalls and reckons, but shows little emotion. This might complicate Kraus's argument that speeches in character allow boys to display otherwise forbidden (because feminine) emotions.

mouth, Libanius has created a person, behind whom flicker two different states: the woman who fornicates and the woman who is wise. But as an independent agent, she is not sustainably both, even inside the parameters of the exercise.

That is a bold claim, but I argue it is based on what she herself says. Inside the exercise, with the new freedom she has, she elects to put herself under the aegis of another power. She adopts a new goddess as guide and she creates a law she can abide by in the following:

> I purify my mind; I flee Aphrodite; I embrace Athena's good reason. I will post this law on Mount Lebanon, so that it has the force of something written: "Since you are allowed, woman, to have wisdom and to flee the one born of foam, do not offer Aphrodite to me as the origin of your wantonness. This sacred precinct was not set up for wise women to simper in. I know that even the Cyprian flees the insulting marriage, in which one father frequently is unaware of the seed he has planted, and a second father takes over after the first, and the lineages are mixed up, and everything begets impiety." I write these things, I will write these things, and I will use them. Quickly now I will destroy the nasty workplace of the whores.[18]

In quick succession at the start of this passage, the speaker uses three present active indicatives: I purify, I flee, I embrace. These are the actions that turn her away from the desire that previously

---

18. Libanius, Progymnasmata 11.18.3: "ἀλλὰ καθαίρω τὴν γνώμην, φεύγω τὴν Ἀφροδίτην, φιλῶ τῆς Ἀθηνᾶς τὴν ἐπιείκειαν. νόμον ἐν τῷ Λιβάνῳ θήσω τοῦτον, ἵνα τοῦ γράμματος ἔχῃ τὴν δύναμιν· ἐξόν σοι, γύναι, καὶ σωφρονεῖν καὶ φεύγειν τὴν Ἀφρογένειαν μή σου τῆς ἀσελγείας ἀφορμὴν τὴν Ἀφροδίτην προβάλλου μοι. οὐ πέφρακται ταῖς σώφροσιν ἱκετεύειν τέμενος. φεύγει καὶ Κύπρις τὸν γάμον, εὖ οἶδα, τὸν ἐφύβριστον, ὅπου πολλάκις ἀγνοεῖ τὸ σπέρμα πατὴρ ὃ πεφύτευκεν, <καὶ> ὁ δεύτερος τοῦ πρώτου σφετερίζεται καὶ μίσγεται τὰ γένη καὶ πάντα τίκτει δυσσέβειαν. ταῦτα γράφω καὶ γράψω καὶ τούτοις χρήσομαι. Τάχα τῶν ἑταιρῶν ἀνελῶ τὸ πικρὸν ἐργαστήριον."

determined her life. And, in content, they reflect the ongoing ripples of the effect of her new wisdom in action. She says she is purifying her mind (and let's note, she actually has one to purify now). To do that, she rejects the influence of one goddess and turns to seek the influence of another. Even when she is self-determined, she recognizes the interpenetration of her consciousness with that of a guiding model goddess, who will now inhabit her mind alongside her, making her two in one.

She also places herself under the provision of a law—but it is one that she herself improvises. Thus, the verbal complexity of the exercise grows ever stronger: this woman, who has only just at the start of the exercise taken on a voice and the perspective of a self-determined (or wise) agent, adopts the voice of another, outside herself. She produces a speech within her speech, an elaboration of a new law to rule her actions. That law does not pronounce or declare, as legal discourse might. It alternately instructs and chides her; it attempts to reason with her. The speaking prostitute we hear is the lawmaker, yet the lawmaker stands outside of her and engages her in debate. The pimps who governed her are replaced by a third-person voice that delineates how she should now act, what loyalties she should now honor—a voice that she insists she has written, though of course, we know that "she" has not written any of it.

It is all under a tension that cannot hold; it is doomed from the very start to have a short life. The two states posited for her—fornication and self-possession—stand at odds. Even the conditions of her speech are contrary to fact according to late ancient norms: she cannot narrate a life of vice and also be a reliable witness to events at the same time.[19] Even Libanius, for all his

---

19. As Daryn Lehoux points out, the "easiest way to malign a witness is to show that his manner of life is vicious." See Daryn Lehoux, *What Did the*

talent, cannot maintain the two opposing poles of the prompt and ends up collapsing them into one by the end of the model. Look at how the voice of the law speaks to the speaker directly, calling her what she is now—not pornē, a prostitute, but *gynaika*, a woman. The prompt has asked us for the words of a pornē sōphronēsasa, but the response has given us a different answer: not what she would say in this state of conflict, but what she would turn out to be at the end of it. When the curtain pulls back, when the workshop of the whores begins to fall, the speaker is just a woman after all.

And yet, she is a memorable one, skillfully crafted. She came into existence for Libanius to show his acumen, and for him to pull our boy along toward that acumen, to inspire him to try to do as well as he did in manipulating language to represent experiences he had never had. Having been put together, she does not slip away when the exercise is put to the side. Impossible women like her persist, as icons, as stories, as exemplars. This sounds like speculation on my part—how could a made-up character persist?—but there is a remarkable text from late antiquity that picks up where Libanius left off.

II: ANOTHER ANONYMOUS WOMAN

The woman materialized in Libanius's model exercise lingered, persisting where she could beyond the classroom, in the imagination of the men who were trained to speak in her voice. Libanius's models for classroom exercises were widely read and adopted in late antiquity. A fascinating text from the fifth or sixth century, preserved in a single manuscript from Madrid, builds on

---

Romans Know? An Inquiry into Science and Worldmaking (University of Chicago Press, 2012), 98.

one by reporting this same woman's experience at a later date. This writer had certainly studied Libanius's model response for the wise prostitute, so I'll call it the *Anonymous Sequel*.[20] But instead of just composing another answer to the same prompt the fourth-century teacher had used, taking up the question, "What would the prostitute come to her senses say?" (*tinas an eipoi logous pornē sōphronēsasa*) this author marks his work as a different genre, perhaps a declamation, by identifying the speaker and those to whom she is speaking: *pornē sōphronēsasa pros tous pariontas autēn erastas*. Not a question, but a statement—a title: "The prostitute who has become wise, to her pursuing lovers."[21] In just a few pages of Greek, this writer—very likely a Christian and perhaps a teacher, or maybe just a grown man reflecting on his past writing exercises—creates a kind of sequel for the woman Libanius had conjured. Here we pick up her story after time has passed and she is on different ground.

It is now a battleground that she occupies. This woman, having come to her senses long ago, has struggled. She begins speaking wearily. "Again the time has come for erotic battles," she says, "again the terrible demon who has resented me wages war against *sōphrosynē*."[22] The repetition in these lines—*palin . . . palin* (again . . . again)—draws us to her standpoint: she has

20. Eugenio Amato, ed., *Severus Sophista Alexandrinus: Progymnasmata quae extant omnia* (De Gruyter, 2009), liii.
21. *Severus Progymnasmata*, 81. Based on this difference, I'm interested that Amato identified the text as an instance of *ethopoeia*; it does not follow the generic form for the title of such an exercise. (Amato titles it in Latin *anonymi ethopoeia meretrices redemptae*; I prefer "Anonymous Sequel.") I am grateful to Michail Kitsos, who first translated this speech and without whose work I would not have realized the significance of the text to my argument.
22. *Anonymous Sequel* 1, in *Severus Progymnasmata*, ed. Amato, 81. Here he identifies an allusion to a letter by Gregory of Nazianzus, one of many. The author of the text very clearly has familiarity with Christian literature.

already been through the wars, and they are starting up once again, and we are due to hear about their terrible constraints. The opening lines also prime us to read in her account a plot that pervades late ancient Christian literature. By naming her situation a "battle" and invoking the presence of a bellicose demon, the speaker seems to narrate for herself the well-known situation of a monk or a holy man: intent on his own discipline, he is tempted, often thwarted, by a demon who enters his very thoughts, planting suggestions and doubt to redirect his good intentions.[23]

A monk's struggle is to master these thoughts and thus to defeat demons. Hers, though, is different. This woman retains the quality of sōphrosynē; her mind and good intentions are intact, and although the demon has attempted to penetrate her thoughts, it has failed. So, just as she managed to preserve herself from licentiousness (*aselgias*), the demon evolved "to invent a new method for the job," which, she says, "seems to me even harder to bear" than the demon's older strategies.[24] As she explains, "Because he could not get me to waver from the wise things I set out to do, he seems to have armed others against us."[25] She already managed to defeat the demon on the battleground where so many monks had struggled and some had even lost, so the demon chose another approach—not her mind, which was resolutely wise, but her environs, the people around her. In these few short words, the opening places this woman at a level above what most early Christian holy men had to manage.[26]

---

23. David Brakke, *Demons and the Making of the Monk: Spiritual Combat in Early Christianity* (Harvard University Press, 2006).
24. *Anonymous Sequel* 1 (*Severus Progymnasmata*, 81).
25. *Anonymous Sequel* 1 (*Severus Progymnasmata*, 81).
26. In this way, the author moves her speech out of the genre of typed speech in character, as there is no conflict within her. The conflict in fact resides outside her.

Unlike most monks, though, her problem is not with the self. The transformation she had at one point undergone, developing sōphrosynē, the very characteristic itself an expression of agency, seemed like it would be enough to change her circumstances. Yet it was fruitless. As she reflects:

> Back then, it did not seem impossible to protect my intention. But as I hauled myself out of those devotedly evil deeds—using that very good intent of mind so that I would not fall back down into them—I never quite made it. What happened!?[27]

Just intending to do well was not enough; neither was actually doing well. Although she had managed to change her life, although she practiced wise deeds, the needle did not move, did not even twitch. As she laments, "everyone still figured that I was worthless."[28] As much as she tries, the esteem of others remains low, and she repeats the lament: "all people categorized me as shameful." Even though she acts differently, the people around her do not. Her hell still lies with other people.

The judgment of others about her past life is so strong that it overrides every other social input those around her might receive. Her basic status is ignored. She was "first among many with respect to fortune, nature, and class," "born a free woman." Even so, she was "hated by those who birthed me and those to whom I belonged, so hated that because of me nature itself was to be denied."[29] Those things that might normally induce one to think well of another person—the inalienable status of rank and family—never worked in her case. What's worse, even her evident practice did not change others' minds. She renders concisely

---

27. *Anonymous Sequel 2* (*Severus Progymnasmata*, 81).
28. *Anonymous Sequel 2* (*Severus Progymnasmata*, 81).
29. *Anonymous Sequel 2* (*Severus Progymnasmata*, 81).

the paradox of being permanently misjudged: "I am the 'architect' of many evil things, even when I have frequently had no part in them; and when I manage to do the best things, I am judged to be no good."[30] This is the fundamental disconnect and alienation of being stereotyped. Regardless of what she does, or what intimacy she may have with her viewers, she is to them still just one thing, a pornē, and thus capable of only evil.

Being typed this way is already its own kind of harm. Beyond that, though, the speech registers the real social consequences of typing, as others' opinions of this woman place limits on her. She has trouble making associations that benefit her, because people disdain her on sight. As a result, "the only refuge for me are the mindless and the profligate—frankly, all those men whom no one would actually approach for anything good."[31] She is stuck, "short on loving, decent men," and so she has to settle. The bad men she is forced to deal with—"cruel critics of things hoped for, even crueler judges of things that have taken place"—put her in the terrible position of having to meet their pleasures just for basic protection. "The absolute worst," she laments, "is having to acquiesce to them, to humor them in all things, and to never do anything they do not like."[32] The limits originate with her lovers and the men she might depend on, but they apply wherever she happens to go. She knows it deeply, asserting, "it is clear this is happening to us, too: priests shut us out and scare us off from the divine word however they can." The very place where a reformed prostitute, a woman committed to sōphrosynē, might find welcome and like-mindedness, among people who recognize redemption and repentance as goods, even sacraments—I mean

30. *Anonymous Sequel 2* (*Severus Progymnasmata*, 82).
31. *Anonymous Sequel 2* (*Severus Progymnasmata*, 82).
32. *Anonymous Sequel 3* (*Severus Progymnasmata*, 82).

the church—is the place from which she is shooed away like a pest. There is no place that accepts her new—or, by the time of this speech, not so new but still improved—self.

The author of the *Anonymous Sequel* provides a remarkably astute account of the ramifications of reputation and even stereotype. We hear in the speech the frustration and disillusionment of this woman who has changed herself and her ways and seen no change reflected back at her. Her description of the problem leads us through a tour of the hierarchy of social value she inhabits, seeing just how shut off she is from possibility, ease, and benefit, exactly the things that philosophers promise will come when one dedicates himself to sōphrosynē. This author—familiar with the prostitute-become-wise, perhaps having written a speech or two for her—grasps that the kind of promise made to the young man of the philosopher's circle will not be kept for women who come to the same realizations. The imagined speech is genuinely the most ethically complex late ancient text I have encountered, with respect to gender, to sociability, to the powers of exclusion.

This text resonates with other passages from ancient Christian literature that are hailed as eerily perceptive, fascinating, and worthy of extensive scholarly reflection. I am thinking of Paul's famous dilemma, of not doing what he wants to do and doing what he does not want to do, or Augustine's recounting of his boyhood desires to steal other people's pears.[33] Of course, both of these men actually did the bad things they worried about, though we count

---

33. I think Paul and Augustine seem preternaturally aware of human psychology to readers who encounter them because their passages are canonical and the seed of a certain culture that the reader has acquired without knowing its origin. When you encounter the seeding text, it seems to confirm what you know, but it works like the Bene Gesserit seeding of culture to other worlds in *Dune*.

them as exemplars for their later ethical development. This hypothetical woman has not—at least, not since her transformation—but as she discovers, she is still caught, not in the act but in the lingering appearance of her past self, and thus discounted. What is worse, she absolutely knows the score, baldly asking, "What should we do? Even if we have sōphrosynē, nobody will believe it."[34] She knows, "I wouldn't get equal treatment even if I lived according to wisdom and in a manner that pleased you."[35] She is resigned, saying, "Because of all this I am prepared never again to give mind to such people."[36] The social awareness and psychological acumen on display are stunningly perceptive.

And yet it is all an act. For as meticulous and insightful as this speech is, it was very likely not a woman who wrote it. It was most probably a rhetorician, practicing the thing he had been taught to do—namely, making a speech to represent what another human being would think about being called a pornē, and what she might experience if that label stuck. Frankly, the speech is densely packed with striking observations, so many more than I have cited here, and it is ripe for more readings based in gender or other sociological analytics. (Indeed, another reading that several smart people have pointed out to me is to take this as a woman's composition! Would, then, the author be a former sex worker come to her senses, or just a woman trained in rhetoric who was taking on that persona, much like her fellow students did?) The prime question for me is: How can a person think this deeply about the effects of stigmatization so as to write this speech, working so closely with its effects as to give

---

34. *Anonymous Sequel* 5 (*Severus Progymnasmata*, 82).
35. *Anonymous Sequel* 4 (*Severus Progymnasmata*, 82).
36. *Anonymous Sequel* 4 (*Severus Progymnasmata*, 82). Alternate translation: "Because of all this, I am out of fucks to give."

voice to the frustrations of the person who experiences it, and *not* somehow come to the conclusion that the situation is terribly unjust and needs to change?

III: EMPATHY OR MASTERY?

Simply reading this one *Anonymous Sequel* might seem like it would foster a sense of empathy; the effect could be even stronger for the person who did the work to compose it. The work of creating such a speech was to imagine oneself as people who were hemmed in or hampered, whether men who found themselves in terrible situations or, in up to one third of the instances, women in different, also terrible situations.[37] Boys learning to write were to visualize for themselves, then to make real for others, a person who was at odds, either with their own expectations (in the case of a character from myth or literature who had come up against something they had not foreseen) or with others' expectations for them (in the case of a generic kind of person, like our wise prostitute). To practice conjuring agency for a person who, in life or in the parameters of the exercise, was defined by their *lack* of agency, would be to stretch a boy's mind. If we zoom out to imagine the widespread assignment of speeches in character as a whole, across hundreds of rhetorical classrooms, over centuries, we see that this activity could have created a groundswell of empathy for others across the ancient world. Doing so just once may have already had some effect on a boy's perspective on the world, but doing so over and over again, each elite boy in rhetorical training attempting it for multiple subjects, could have

---

37. See the catalog assembled in Amato and Ventrella, "L'éthopée dans la pratique scolaire et littéraire."

developed in him a real sense of what it felt like to be powerless, or without options. And that might have ushered in a very different political landscape for the ancient world.

But no, that is not what happened. The historical record shows no revolution in social relations following this widespread custom of wondering what others would say when faced with difficulty and then writing about it. Laborers stayed marked by their trades; enslavement continued throughout the late ancient period; women remained subject to the strictures that bound their lives—all while this seeming exercise in empathy, speech in character, continued to be practiced by every boy who, as a man, would take an office or write a book.[38] The rhetorical classroom was not, despite its evident potential, an engine of solidarity with others.

In fact, it was the opposite. First, practices of identifying with others are notoriously difficult to do, particularly when the other with whom we are to identify is a real individual person and not a literary character.[39] Second, first-person ventriloquization, when performed by the powerful to represent the less powerful, does not challenge the social hierarchies that allow it in the first place. Scholar of American history Saidiya V. Hartman analyzed the nineteenth-century practice, by white abolitionists, of ventriloquizing enslaved Black people; those with power and freedom to write took up the pen to pretend to speak as the powerless, for the purpose of showcasing just how unjust slavery was. And yet, as Hartman teases out the assumptions that would allow

---

38. For the endurance of these social arrangements, see Sarah E. Bond, *Trade and Taboo: Disreputable Professions in the Roman Mediterranean* (University of Michigan Press, 2016).

39. Elaine Scarry, "The Difficulty of Imagining Other Persons," in *The Handbook of Interethnic Coexistence*, ed. Eugene Weiner (Continuum, 1998).

a white writer to take this on, empathy recedes further and further from view as a possible outcome.

Consider the situation of John Rankin, who wanted to show that Black people were human beings, their suffering as deep and painful as what a white person would experience under the same circumstances. He "narrates an imagined scenario in which he, along with his wife and child, is enslaved."[40] As Hartman unpacks his attempt to speak as another, she explains that his "flight of imagination and slipping into the captive's body unlatches a Pandora's box and, surprisingly, what comes to the fore is the difficulty and slipperiness of empathy."[41] Rankin, like other white abolitionist writers such as Harriet Beecher Stowe, wished to give voice to the enslaved by speaking *as* them, in their voices displaying the suffering they faced and pleading for others to recognize it. Yet, as Hartman explains, "in making the other's suffering one's own, this suffering is occluded by the other's obliteration."[42] Rankin's attempt, well-intentioned though it might be, does not bring the experience of the other home to be understood, but rather "exacerbates the distance between readers and those suffering by literally removing the slave from view as pain is brought close."[43]

Most disturbing, ventriloquization of the other ends up participating in the same exchanges of use and pleasure that the act of ownership in slaving does. In both cases, "the captive body" is "an abstract and empty vessel vulnerable to the project of others'

---

40. Saidiya V. Hartman, *Scenes of Subjection: Terror, Slavery, and Self-Making in Nineteenth-Century America*, Race and American Culture (Oxford University Press, 1997), 18.
41. Hartman, *Scenes of Subjection*, 18.
42. Hartman, *Scenes of Subjection*, 19.
43. Hartman, *Scenes of Subjection*, 20.

feelings, ideas, desires, and values"—as if it is there merely to be the container for Rankin's exercise.[44] Nineteenth-century American slavery is distant, in time and in magnitude, from the ventriloquization that late ancient boys participated in as a part of their rhetorical training. Hartman's analysis is nevertheless resonant, since she shows the sense of propriety it takes to speak as, or speak for, someone else. Over the long term, any adoption of the voice of a less powerful person—even when seemingly well-intentioned by the adopter—is no generosity, creates no empathy. Instead, it is, as Hartman writes, consistently "entangled" with the same constellations of power and violence that create the differential being exercised in the first place.

In the case of the boys who practice these speeches, there is no indication that their exercises were even intended to benefit those for whom they spoke. The prospect is all the more absurd because they were *boys*, raised in elite families. If they had scant experience of the world because of their youth, they had even less experience of what it is like to be powerless, because of their station. How could a rhetorical student possibly know what a prostitute come to her senses would say? And yet the student who had been assigned this speech, who had composed and practiced it, and who had heard his teacher and perhaps the other students praise his efforts once completed, could leave the classroom sure of the congruence of his ideas—his sense of what that impossible woman would think and say and do, and the reality of others in the world.

Instead of empathy, then, the practice of speaking this way teaches a boy the disposition of mastery: that his thoughts and

---

44. Hartman, *Scenes of Subjection*, 21. And Rankin's use, Hartman wonders, could have itself involved pleasure, as he gave in to the widespread and common "desire to don, occupy, or possess blackness or the black body as a sentimental resource."

assumptions, however inexpert, are sufficient to the task of knowing others.[45] His resources, however meager, are adequate, and he knows this because his teacher and his classmates tell him so. Trying to speak convincingly as a woman meant sounding like what your teacher and maybe your classmates—likely none of them women—thought a woman sounded like.[46] The form and the environment where he practiced being someone else encouraged play, not perception; the products of the boy's play are accurate and universal, according to his social equals. Then, upon meeting a woman (a fornicating woman, sure, but as I have pointed out, that could be any one of us), he knows what she is thinking, what she is, because he has thought like her. No, he has *been* her.

And of course, as I have said, these women persist outside the classroom. This one did, certainly. An author imagined her later, and in a distinct location: just on the border of a Christian community, attempting to enter that community. She was denied access, but he clearly had it; the allusions and echoes in the *Anonymous Sequel* speech reflect the mind of a well-read Christian.

IV: THE WOMAN ON THE EDGE

The same impossible woman makes an appearance in another late ancient text. This time, she is not in a model exercise but has been translated to a different genre: Christian hagiography. The

---

45. And this is in contrast to the skepticism, particularly of one's thoughts and impressions, that is cultivated in late ancient philosophical classrooms.

46. This fact has huge implications for the "women" we find in the late ancient archive, especially those represented in first-person voice. See Julia Hillner, "Empresses, Queens, and Letters: Finding a 'Female Voice' in Late Antiquity?" *Gender & History* 31 (2019): 353–82; Ellen Muehlberger, "Perpetual Adjustment: The *Passion of Perpetua and Felicity* and the Entailments of Authenticity," *JECS* 30 (2022): 313–42.

Life of Mary of Egypt is difficult to date with precision, but it was cited by another Christian writer in the eighth century, so most readers locate its origin in the seventh century.[47] That date would roughly square with ancient estimations, which assign authorship to Sophronius, a bishop of Jerusalem in the 630s.[48] In the *Life*, an anonymous narrator introduces a monk named Zosimus, who, after arriving at middle age, started to seek out newer, more extreme models of pious discipline for himself. He had been disappointed, thinking there was no more greater challenge to take on, and he wondered, "Is there a monk on earth . . . who can show me a kind of asceticism I have not accomplished? Is there a man to be found in the desert who has surpassed me?"[49]

As it turns out, there was another person who had surpassed him, but *she* was not easy to find. Zosimus traveled for many years, joining a new monastery and eventually leaving it to move into the wilderness beyond the River Jordan, before he encountered Mary, a former prostitute, who reluctantly gives up her life story to him after much persuasion. Having lived a dissolute life as a young adult, she had an encounter with the Virgin Mary and began a new path; by the time readers meet her in Zosimus's story, she has been living in the desert for forty-seven years. She leads a feral existence, unclothed, her "body black as if tanned by the scorching of the sun."[50] Almost as soon as he meets her, Zosimus

47. Maria Kouli, "Life of St. Mary of Egypt," in *Holy Women of Byzantium: Ten Saints' Lives in English Translation*, ed. Alice-Mary Talbot (Dumbarton Oaks, 1996), 66.

48. Some, but not all, modern readers agree. See Kouli, "Life of St. Mary of Egypt," 66 and Anne Marie Sargent, "The Penitent Prostitute: The Tradition and Evolution of the 'Life of St. Mary the Egyptian'" (PhD diss., University of Michigan, 1977). The latter has an exhaustive discussion of ancient and modern opinions about the text and its author.

49. *Life of Mary of Egypt* 3, trans. Kouli, *Holy Women of Byzantium*, 72.

50. *Life of Mary of Egypt* 10, trans. Kouli, *Holy Women of Byzantium*, 76.

realizes that Mary has surpassed him; after he gets her story, she remains in the desert, while he retreats back to the safety of his monastery.

A saint, and an unconventional one, this Mary could not be further from the regimented, homosocial culture of the rhetorical classroom. Yet she is one more incarnation of the same imagined woman we have already met. To prove it, let me show you her components. The figure of a woman dedicated to religious practice and inhabiting the desert to renounce sexual temptation appears in multiple late ancient Christian texts. Cyril of Scythopolis wrote about a Mary who lived by herself in a cave in the desert, having absented her church in the city when men paid her too much attention; she lived eighteen years on the food and water she brought with her, before she was eventually found dead and buried by another monk.[51] There is another woman in a late ancient text, who moved out of the city to hide in a cave after having had a relationship with a male monk; she lived naked, surviving thirty years on the food and water she carried with her, and she too was later entombed by traveling monks when she was found dead.[52] There is a shorter account of a similar woman in John Moschus's *Spiritual Meadow*: another penitent woman flees sexual temptation, surviving unsheltered in the desert on only the things she carried.[53] All these tales so closely align with the

---

51. Kouli, *Holy Women of Byzantium*, 65; Benedicta Ward, *Harlots of the Desert: A Study in Repentance in Early Monastic Sources* (Cistercian, 1987), 28–29.

52. Ward, *Harlots of the Desert*, 29–32, has the whole text in translation.

53. And there are still others along these lines. Cf. *Acts of Thomas* 51–54, discussed by Meghan R. Henning in *Hell Hath No Fury: Gender, Disability, and the Invention of Damned Bodies in Early Christian Literature* (Yale University Press, 2021); and Ross Shepard Kraemer, *Unreliable Witnesses: Religion, Gender, and History in the Greco-Roman Mediterranean* (Oxford University Press, 2012), 34–42.

pattern that is taken up in the *Life of Mary of Egypt*, the repentant woman in the wild (and sometimes named Mary), that scholars of that text have often seen in them predecessors of Mary of Egypt, whether as earlier narrations that tell the story of the same character or as literary sources that were tapped to create the tale of the Egyptian saint.[54]

Yet the *Life of Mary of Egypt* is far wilder, and bolder, than these predecessors, in part because it has drawn on another imaginative vein that they had not used. Within Mary is the figure of the prostitute come to her senses, taken as an inspiration and a template for her character. In this *Life*, the holy woman in the desert speaks prolifically, revealing much more of herself than the other women like her, telling stories that go beyond a bit of miraculously extended food or rugged perseverance.[55] The long account she gives Zosimus of her life, its twists and turns, could easily be slotted in as an answer to Libanius's prompt, "What would a prostitute come to her senses say?" The components of her speech follow the genre: she traces her past, laments it, tells of the change she underwent and her feelings about that change, and even makes the predictable observations about how "unbelievable" her story is.[56]

And it *is* an extraordinary story, from an extraordinary woman. The repentance she had undertaken is far more extensive

54. Kouli (*Holy Women of Byzantium*) takes them as earlier reports of the same historical subject's life, while Ward (*Harlots of the Desert*) allows that the earlier texts might just be sources adopted to create the new life of Mary of Egypt.

55. Just the fact that so much of the text—almost half—is Mary's speech is remarkable in the context of Christian expectations of modesty for holy women. On which, see Wilkinson, "The Modest Mouth," in *Women and Modesty*, 86–116.

56. *Life of Mary of Egypt* 21. Cf. the opening narrative of Zosimus, which uses *apiston* specifically.

than that of any other Christian saint or even character from late ancient literature. She was, she tells Zosimus, absolutely devoted to lewd, lascivious actions, seeking out fornication as frequently as possible. She was barely a prostitute, in that she specifically did not seek out sex for money—for cash, she begged and she spun, but sex was a simple want. "The truth is," she admits, "I had an insatiable passion and [an] uncontrollable lust to wallow in filth."[57] Her desires rule over others' wishes: when she talks her way onto a ship full of men about to set sail, she confesses that she "forced these wretched men into acts against their will."[58] This Mary teaches *sailors* how to be filthy!

She used to do a million debauched things, and, from that depth, she soars to new heights, quite literally. Just after she meets Zosimus, and long after her repentance, he observes her praying. She is intent, and he idly thinks that she has been praying for a long time; when he looks at her, she is levitating, "hanging in the air" above the ground.[59] Even with this kind of evidence, though, Zosimus doubts whether she is holy, and thinks she might be some kind of spirit. Later in the story, she displays other abilities impossible to misinterpret, as she walks on water to cross the River Jordan, not once but twice.[60] She is not on a stormy sea, but she is managing the doubt of those around her the same way that Jesus did on the sea, by stepping out onto the surface of the waters. The change she has undergone is practically impossible—as remarkable as the woman in Libanius's model answer, and perhaps more so, as she is not just a prostitute come to her senses but a prostitute who has become so holy, so Christlike, as to walk on water.

57. *Life of Mary of Egypt* 18.
58. *Life of Mary of Egypt* 21.
59. *Life of Mary of Egypt* 15.
60. *Life of Mary of Egypt* 35, 36.

The speech Mary delivers in her *Life* goes beyond simple transformation, in this respect echoing the *Anonymous Sequel*, too, so much so that it could *also* bear the title given to that short Spanish text: "The prostitute come to her senses, to her pursuing lovers." Zosimus gets her story, after all, by hounding her, going out to the desert, then following her over her protests. She walks away, and, as Peter Mena so concisely puts it, "And still he chases after her."[61] Mary has what he desires, and he begs for her story, asking her to lay bare her inner knowledge. He even invokes divine approval for his unwelcomed pursuit: if God had not wanted her to tell him her story, he would not have allowed Zosimus to find her.[62]

But, like the woman in the *Anonymous Sequel*, Mary of Egypt experiences constant frustration. Although Zosimus has left behind one monastery, then another, to find Mary and learn from her, the invisible hierarchy of the church has followed him into the desert, and it contains their relationship. Indeed, Mary is not in that hierarchy, but constantly outside it. She is reformed, so sanctified as to outperform any ascetic, yet she still wanders the desert, undisciplined, with none but this wandering monk to include her in the church's rituals. Even the one time she did enter a church in her life was fraught and over quickly. Mary's repentance was spurred by a brush with a church building. While she was not yet wise, she attempted to follow a crowd in for the festival of the exaltation of the cross. On the threshold, she can see other participants inside, but something keeps her out:

> I tried to join the crowd and force my way to the entrance, pushing forward but being pushed back. Eventually, with great trouble and

---

61. Peter Anthony Mena, *Place and Identity in the Lives of Antony, Paul, and Mary of Egypt: Desert as Borderland*, Religion and Spatial Studies (Palgrave Macmillan, 2019), 92.

62. *Life of Mary of Egypt* 16.

grief—wretched woman that I am—I approached the door through which one entered the church . . . But as soon as I stepped on the threshold of the door, all the other people entered unhindered, while some kind of divine power held me back . . . though the church received the others without any obstacle, it refused entrance to me alone, miserable woman that I am; and just as if a large company of soldiers were arrayed for this purpose, with orders to prevent my entering, so did some kind of overwhelming power hold me back and once more I was standing in the courtyard.[63]

Mary is hindered by the church itself, barred from entering by a force bigger than she is. Twice she labels herself—miserable woman, wretched woman—and those labels point to what is wrong. The church does not want to accept her, not because she is a sinful person but because she is sinful *woman*. Waiting tearfully in the courtyard, she encounters the Virgin, who tells her to repent, but then tells her that the desert (and not the church) is the place for her.[64] Off she goes, never to return.[65] Like the woman in the Spanish text, she has repented and changed, but the people and structures around her never recognize it.

It may seem odd to think that the saint in such a popular hagiography is a literary creation shaped by practice exercises for boys, but the image of the impossible woman is indelible, the pull of her suspended repentance almost irresistible to the men who want to represent women. If there is any doubt that Mary in this *Life* speaks with a ventriloquized voice—that she is yet another instance of a man imagining the impossible woman—the narrative details of her story can clue us in. In the story, we only hear her voice because Zosimus has made it possible. When Mary first meets Zosimus, she warns him that she cannot talk to

63. *Life of Mary of Egypt* 22. This is abridged.
64. *Life of Mary of Egypt* 23.
65. *Life of Mary of Egypt* 25.

him because she is naked, and she turns away. He then shares his cloak so she can speak. Ostensibly, this is about modesty, but the scenario shows us a woman literally taking on the mantle of a visiting man so that she can tell her story.[66]

Other details point the same direction. For instance, at their first meeting, Mary and Zosimus are locked in an odd choreography, mirroring each other as they kneel; they then prostrate themselves before she eventually speaks. When she does give him what he wants, she signals her acquiescence, saying, "since we are commanded to be obedient, I shall willingly do your bidding." It is at his wish that she talks. But, when she happens to be praying by herself, he cannot make out her words, because she mumbles and, as the text goes on to relate, "her voice was not heard to utter articulate sounds."[67] These details all do their own work within the frame of the story, but we can also read them as allusions to the situation of its composition. This "woman" cannot be clearly heard without the man who draws out her voice; the bare fact that this saint's life can be read at all points in this direction, since we know about Mary of Egypt only because Zosimus went to find her and because he recites her story for her.

Having been created by drawing on earlier monastic stories and patterned on the persistent figure of the prostitute come to her senses, this Mary is a new incarnation of the impossible woman. Repeated once in this *Life*, she ripples out from it, meeting readers in multiple copies of the text, in new versions of the story and new translations.[68] Mary meets a new cadre of readers

---

66. *Life of Mary of Egypt* 12.
67. *Life of Mary of Egypt* 15.
68. Extremely popular, the text survives in more than one hundred manuscripts, and was quickly translated into Latin, Syriac, Armenian, and Ethiopic (see Sargent, "Penitent Prostitute," 1). Benedicta Ward's introduction

in each new version, but she also lives outside these replications by continuing on in the imagination of those readers. Caroline T. Schroeder wrote of another Christian heroine, Melania, showing that she could be "separated from her original surroundings and drawn into a much more intimate affective relationship with the audiences of her *Life*," and the same should be true of Mary of Egypt.[69] That is to say, characters never stay just characters but live on to influence how readers think and act—something true for literature in general but doubly so for didactic literature like hagiography. As Reyhan Durmaz observes, "narratives gave conceptual texture to interpersonal and intercultural relations" in the premodern world, and the story of the impossible woman we encounter in Mary of Egypt is no different.[70]

CONCLUSION: RESILIENT IGNORANCE

In *Power and Persuasion in Late Antiquity*—itself a book based on a series of lectures—Peter Brown brought attention to the system of learning I have described here and, with his spotlight of narrative skill, drew readers to understand how deeply Mediterranean politics were shaped by what young boys practiced in those classrooms.[71] The scope of the book, though, drew a circle around

---

to the text makes clear the popularity and broad reception of the *Life* (see *Harlots of the Desert*). And, of course, hookers with a heart of gold persist: see Julia Roberts' character in *Pretty Woman*.

69. Caroline T. Schroeder, "Exemplary Women," in *Melania: Early Christianity through the Life of One Family*, ed. Catherine Michael Chin and Caroline T. Schroeder (University of California Press, 2017), 18.

70. Reyhan Durmaz, *Stories between Christianity and Islam: Saints, Memory, and Cultural Exchange in Late Antiquity and Beyond* (University of California Press, 2022), 1.

71. Peter Brown, *Power and Persuasion in Late Antiquity: Towards a Christian Empire*, The Curti Lectures (University of Wisconsin, 1992).

the boy, now the man, and the ways that the education system enabled *his* career, affected *his* trajectory. Of course, it may be natural for historians to identify with the boy in the classroom, for a multitude of reasons. First, this boy is being trained in writing; historians are writers, after all, and we were all once students trying to develop our skills in composition and persuasion. Also, the boys who practiced these exercises became writers as adults, which means they left behind some trace of their intellectual activity in the historical record. When scholars attempt to represent the past, we inevitably see more significance where there is more documentation, and the boys who trained in the rhetorical curriculum produced most (all?) of the texts available to us as we make the attempt.

The salience of these boys in what we read and know does not mean that others did not exist and live and suffer and thrive in the late ancient world. Historians will gesture to that fact, but we are often at a loss for how to know about those others, how to write about them, how to tell their stories. Ross Kraemer has detailed the inscrutable character of ancient sources about women, and sometimes, when scholars encounter ideas about women in ancient texts, they read them as reflections on men.[72] Even this essay, for example, is not about anyone but the boy in the classroom, and the men that such boys grew up to be. You might say I am speaking for the boy, imagining him and taking on his voice, but the boy in these classrooms becomes a man whose voice we hear in the archive of literature from the ancient world. Watching that boy learn, seeing how he was directed to know others by being others, the ease he is given to speak as another—all of this confirms what Carolyn Kay Steedman observed, that educational

---

72. Kraemer, *Unreliable Witnesses*.

materials are not just sources for themselves but are a window onto the broader, most influential structures in a culture.[73]

All memorable characters persist, but they especially endure in the minds that created them. In the case of the prostitute come to her senses, boys were creating her anew each time, and the story they made for her past would form part of their memories, too, doubling as theirs *and* hers. There are glimpses of how the specific woman in our sample exercise may have persisted, to arise again as the subject of a sequel, or a saint's life. We can draw a line linking her appearances from Constantinople in the fourth century, over to somewhere in Spain in the fifth or sixth, and back to Jerusalem in the seventh.[74] Those texts are, of course, not the only places she existed. Instead, their singular snapshots capture a larger and longer distribution, where she is imagined, practiced, revisited, and retouched by writing boys and men.[75] There was a certain pleasure in returning to visit the prostitute once again, creating something impossible and yet under one's control.

In part because of that pleasure, she lives on, available as a memorable example and shared reference point among the men who had practiced speaking in her voice as boys. Daryn Lehoux has written about the way that examples held in mind can change a line of logic, even in the most austerely logical of discussions, creating an effect of what he gently labels "observational selectivity"

---

73. Carolyn Steedman, "Mother Made Conscious: The Historical Development of a Primary School Pedagogy," *History Workshop Journal* 20 (1985): 150.

74. Compare the monk's story in Socrates, *Church History* 4.23, too.

75. This is a confirmation of Amy Richlin's estimation that women in ancient sources are almost always the product of men's imaginations. See Amy Richlin, *Arguments with Silence: Writing the History of Roman Women* (University of Michigan Press, 2014).

that belies the comprehension of unforeseen information.[76] Memorizing a speech in character, or creating one, implants an enduring form of the woman and her experience, and whatever new information might strike a boy about a woman, or a prostitute, may not land because of the prevalence and the realistic effect of the model that has already been installed in him and his peers. To call this a stereotype is not exactly sufficient, because it is a matter of the boy having taken on someone else's subjectivity, taking in her experience as he has conjured it, and being taken seriously when he presents it to others. Every time he uses the exemplar, he can look around to his old classmates, now men, to see if he has made something that strikes them as "real." If they agree—and why wouldn't they?—then he has comprehended correctly and nothing need change.[77]

There results a kind of presumptive arrogance about knowing others: a type of scrim forms between him and the world, painted with traces of the woman he has pretended to be. The scrim will take any information he might have comprehended about a woman he encounters—signs of her independence, her agency, her humanity—and blurs it behind the much sharper image of the woman he has been. Data that might challenge his model is epistemologically ephemeral, slippery, unlikely to put a dent in the image he has in his mind or even stick in the memory of the boy, or man. His interactions with anyone in a class of person that he has at one point spoken for can then just be made to cohere with his prior experience, rather than depart from it. In this way, speech in

---

76. What one holds as a norm or model affects what can be seen or known. See Lehoux, *What Did the Romans Know?* 83–98.

77. That reinforcement is part of why dominant cultures return to performing the roles of the less powerful again and again, to show it to themselves as reality. See Hartman, *Scenes of Subjection*.

character is a *hindrance* to the formation of knowledge, if by that we mean seeking an as-accurate-as-possible sense of another's experience. Pretending to be women who were people was a performative part of a machine that generated ignorance of women's real condition. Indeed, that machine was outside the pathways of legal definition; it preceded those pathways that conferred legal personhood, from property rights and inheritance rights to witness credibility and protection from vulnerability.[78] This machine was the accumulation of processes and practices outside the legal that *also* created and maintained status, at least as powerful and perhaps even more powerful than laws that did so.[79]

What is created is a resilient ignorance, constituted not by a lack of facts but by a buffer against facts that can withstand multiple encounters with the challenging peculiarities of individuals.[80] Where the wise prostitute appeared, whether in text or in mind, she blotted out others. It may be methodologically naïve to say, but I venture that women in antiquity were people and had self-possession; statistically, they should have been as important to the creation and maintenance of culture as men. Yet the writers I study were able to work their entire intellectual lives without ever entertaining that idea seriously. Speech in character was practice in *not* seeing the types of people one finds in

78. These are the markers of agency in post-Enlightenment liberalism, but they were all granted to only *some* human beings in the time period I am discussing.

79. See Scarry, "Difficulty of Imagining Other Persons," 45: "The human capacity to injure other people has always been much greater than its ability to imagine other people."

80. Cf. "ways of knowing," which should be studied alongside "ways of unknowing." Here I am taking up the charge given by Charles Mills to investigate the maintenance of ignorance as closely as we investigate the maintenance of knowledge. See Charles Mills, *The Racial Contract* (Cornell University Press, 1997).

everyday life, and it came with the benefit of never incurring a political liability to take them as equal others worthy of regard. And it worked. The boy's training was a central plank in the scaffolding of power relations maintained in the ancient world—not because of how he wielded power or persuaded people explicitly but in the way he managed to avoid learning of the humanity and agency of others all around him.

It was all the more lasting for how pleasurable it may have been. There is a small thrill in watching an impossible thing be true, and a bigger one in knowing that you created the impossible thing. Ancient writers (and modern ones) do love an exceptional case of agency, particularly when they are the ones to conjure it. With the prostitute who has come to her senses, it is not as if writers did not understand that a woman, or a prostitute, could possibly have wisdom. It is that they like to watch as the rule that she cannot possibly have wisdom is enforced—paradoxically, in the exploration of the contrary. It is not as if they did not recognize that others outside the elite male class could have agency—their plays and poems are filled with anxiety about what happens when the enslaved members of households start to plan, or when women conspire. Speeches in character were not written in antiquity for subjects like rocks or clouds. They were written for people who surely were recognized, on some level, as having the capacities granted to them in the exercise, and then the thrill came in the puzzle: that social structures did *not* recognize this fact, and that the boy writing the speech was the master of all the rules. And, because speeches in character have no resolution, the thrill that comes in working them over has to be their central feature. There is a pleasure in not solving, in toying, in knowing the woman well enough to speak as her and then leaving her to fade right back out of existence.

CHAPTER TWO

Foundations of Knowledge

Domesticating Evidence of Identity

The late ancient Christian bishop Augustine of Hippo often took up the problem of Christianness in his writing, exploring the potential ways one could know or prove: Who was a Christian? And how thoroughly Christian were they? During Augustine's lifetime, these were already difficult questions to answer, as there was quite a wide variation in what people thought "Christian" signified. But there was also a larger issue. Even if there could be some kind of agreement on what made a Christian, where did the evidence of meeting that standard reside? In his autobiographical work *Confessions*, the bishop's approach to the problem took the form of narrative. That is, he told stories about himself that framed the choices and commitments he had made and, along the way, he told stories about others, too. For instance, Augustine tells the tale of Simplicianus, a Christian who had formed the closest of friendships with a rhetorical teacher and translator, Victorinus.[1]

---

1. *Confessions* 8.2.3, in *Augustine: Confessions*, ed. James J. O'Donnell (Clarendon Press, 1992): "familiarissime noverat," or in English, "he knew him like the closest of family."

Despite not being a member of his friend's church, Victorinus had long been a reader of Christian texts. He had studied the scriptures and all Christian writings diligently, and from them he presumably knew both Christian concepts and Christian narratives of the past. At one point in their friendship, when their respective commitments were again the topic of conversation, Victorinus chided Simplicianus by saying, "You should recognize that I am already a Christian."[2] Simplicianus demurred, saying that he would not consider his friend a Christian until he actually saw him in a church. The teacher of rhetoric volleyed, deadpanning, "So, walls make a Christian, then?"[3]

Within the joke was a serious matter—namely, what was it that qualified a person as a Christian? If not the reading of Christian literature and the study of Christian ideas, could it be having a presence in certain locations? In the story, eventually, Victorinus took actions that qualified him. He took instruction, he entered his name for possible baptism, and finally he gave a profession of faith. In this story, it was not the walls that made the Christian but the rites of passage that granted one entrance to the church, both in a social sense and in a physical sense; as a member of the community, Victorinus was also literally a person let into the building.[4] A membership ritual, administered by other Christians, is what made Victorinus into a Christian, at least in the frame of this vignette.

---

2. *Confessions* 8.2.4: "Dicebat Simpliciano, non palam sed secretius et familiarius: noveris iam me esse christianum." The theme of "familiarity" repeats in this phrase.

3. *Confessions* 8.2.4): "ille autem inridebat dicens, 'ergo parietes faciunt christianos?'"

4. For information about how catechumens had limited access to the rituals and were asked to leave before certain parts of the service, see, e.g., Cyril of Jerusalem's *Catechetical Lectures*.

Stories are often simpler than real life, and late ancient Christian literature registers a range of messy doubts about whether procedures could reliably signal a person's commitment. But of course, something as voluntaristic as "commitment" is not visible. There was no single reliable mark of Christianness in late antiquity. The supposed bedrock of baptism, of confession, even of church attendance—these were all inadequate to guarantee a person's commitment. Doubts persisted in some way and for some persons.

In this chapter, I will first recount the basic points of doubt that late ancient Christians had about how much one could trust the usual signs of initiation, then consider what arose from the manifest insecurity we will see in the surviving literature. When Christians sought surety about the intentions of those they doubted, but for whom they had little tangible evidence, they turned to what may seem a very odd source: the buildings and property associated with the people in doubt. Buildings are significant in late ancient Christian culture for the way they can demonstrate power and wealth, but we will see that they are as much an epistemic repository as an economic one. Their contents come to serve as a "substitute for what cannot be seen" in the person who inhabits them.[5] What cannot be surmised has to be evidenced some other way, and in late antiquity the scope of Christian knowing reached all the way into others' homes and properties. This

---

5. Linda Williams, *Hard Core: Power, Pleasure, and the "Frenzy of the Visible"* (University of California Press, 1989), 95. Here she is speaking about the inability to evidence the female orgasm (an epistemically unstable object if there ever was one!), leading to the hyperfocus in pornography on the visible product of the male orgasm—i.e., the "money shot." Williams's argument inspired my line of thinking about situations of scarce evidence and how matter of one sort can stand in for proof of another.

method of knowing others enabled Christians to think about the exercise of power with new license.

I: DOUBTING CHRISTIANS

During the century after the decriminalization of Christianity, Christian communities grew at a rapid pace, initiating dozens and sometimes hundreds of new members at a time. Preserved in literature from the fourth century are lecture series given to these new initiates, to train them in the discipline that they were joining. The existence of these lessons suggests that there were enough new people interested in becoming members that churches routinized the process for mass use. And indeed, churches were full. For proof, we can return to the testimony of Augustine. Interpreting a verse from the Psalms about how the works of the Lord "multiply beyond number,"[6] the bishop broke it down for his audience: the people in attendance were the works of the Lord. "What great crowds fill the churches!" he said. The crowds were there, active and vital, "pressing against the walls, squeezing and shoving each other, practically suffocating themselves because of how many there are."[7] Some part of this scene may indicate Augustine's talent for imagining what he wanted to be true, but logic dictates that his hyperbole decorated a basic reality any of his contemporaries would recognize. There *were* many more new Christians in his time, many more people seeking initiation, enough that the physical structures of the church did not quite seem adequate to contain them.

6. *Enn. in Ps.* 39.10 (PL 36:440): "multiplicati sunt super numerum."
7. *Enn. in Ps.* 39.10 (PL 36:440): "quantis turbis implentur ecclesiae, stipantur parietes, pressuris se urgent, prope se suffocant multitudine."

Surely a large number of new initiates was a good thing, as the growth of the community was a central goal for Christians. Yet the mere presence of a person inside a church did not necessarily mean anything about him. Working with the same verse from the Psalms in a different context, Augustine had a more jaded view of the proliferation of new Christians. He observed, "there are so many of the faithful gathered together and such crowds run to gather at the church; many are truly converted, many are falsely converted. Those who are truly converted are fewer, and the ones falsely converted outnumber them. This is what 'they are multiplied beyond number' means."[8] Interpreting a different verse from elsewhere in the Psalms, he laid out the problem: "Not everyone" who goes through the process, he wrote, "is so won over as to be actually converted. Many just continue in stubbornness."[9] There is the example of the man who is attached to a *meretrix*—literally, a lying woman, but colloquially, a sex worker, the very same kind of woman who was the subject of so much speechmaking in the ancient classroom. The man is "not taught first to put her aside and then to approach baptism. Instead, [his teachers think,] as he stays involved with her and even confesses—no, professes!—that he plans to stay with her in the future as well, he should be admitted and baptized."[10]

8. *Enn. in Ps.* 39.10 (PL 36:441): "quanti fideles agglomerantur, quantae turbae concurrunt, multi uere conuersi, multi falso conuersi; et pauciores sunt uere conuersi, plures falso conuersi; quia multiplicati sunt super numerum."

9. *Enn. in Ps.* 34.9 (PL 36:328): "non enim omnes sic vincuntur, ut convertantur et credant; multi in pertinacia remanent, multi spiritus praecedendi servant in corde."

10. *De fide et operibus* 1.1 (PL 40:197): "uerbi gratia, si quisquam meretrici adhaeret, non ei prius praecipiatur, ut ab ea discedat et tunc ueniat ad baptismum, sed etiam cum ea manens mansurum que se confitens seu etiam profitens admittatur et baptizetur nec inpediatur fieri membrum christi, etiamsi membrum meretricis esse perstiterit."

This example indicts the man, but it also indicts the church who accepts him. There are Christians who imagined baptism to incur no requirements at all—the person to be baptized is not asked to change his ways. Without a unified understanding among Christian leaders about the strictures of baptism, Christians were put in the position of directing their own approaches. The baptized Christian, thus in charge of his own fate, can, as Augustine wrote, choose to build on the foundation of baptism with "gold and silver and precious stones," or he can build it on "wood, hay, and straw," but he must consider that the edifice he is building—his Christian life—will be tested by fire.[11] With it left to individuals to interpret what baptism required, the guarantee that baptismal status meant anything about a person was thin at best.

Baptism was a wobbly sign of Christian commitment on other terms, too. Even though the proper kind of baptism might be sought, the seeker might have ulterior motives. For example, both narrative and legal texts from late antiquity attempted to address the problem of people who wanted baptism to free them from other responsibilities. Issuances preserved in the *Theodosian Code* address the "deception of hypocrites" who join the community "for the purpose of evading prosecution for crimes and on account of different necessities."[12] Socrates, the church historian, devoted a section of his ecclesiastical history to specifying with examples what people might want to get out of baptism

---

11. *De fide et operibus* 1.1(PL 40:197–98): "saluum eum futurum tamquam per ignem, uelut qui aedificauerit super fundamentum, quod est christus, non aurum, argentum, lapides pretiosos, sed ligna, fenum, stipulam."

12. *CTh.* 16.8.23, in *The Theodosian Code and Novels, and the Sirmondian Constitutions*, ed. and trans., Clyde Pharr et al. (Princeton University Press, 1952], 470. See also Andrew Jacobs's discussion in "'Ad religionis lucem de tenebris superstitionis': Jewish Converts under Christian Law," paper presented at the North American Patristics Society annual meeting, 2018.

beyond just Christian initiation, and the worldly benefits were apparently many.[13] Earlier, Eusebius of Caesarea had addressed the same issue in his *Life of Constantine*, complaining of those who converted for their own interests.[14] Across centuries of late ancient Christian culture, where there was conversion, there was the question of motivation: Was the commitment signaled by catechism and confession and baptism verifiable, and why was it made? What did it get for the new convert? People might stand inside the walls of the church while their hearts remained outside, Augustine warned elsewhere.[15]

Of course, this was a concern that some Christians had with Augustine himself—a sense of doubt about his commitment to Christianity is likely what impelled him to compose his *Confessions* in the first place. Latent questions residing in the community about the ritual of initiation and its ability to reliably indicate someone's Christianness also applied to Augustine. At the end of the fourth century, he had been approached to lead a small community of Christians in North Africa. His writing and speaking ability qualified him for the role—his compatriots wanted someone who could teach and persuade—and his experience made him seem the right choice, in some ways. In others, though,

---

13. Socrates, *Ecclesiastical History* 7.4, 13, 17, 38, all cited by Jacobs, "'Coloured by the Nature of Christianity': Nock's Invention of Religion and Ex-Jews in Late Antiquity," in *Celebrating Arthur Darby Nock: Choice, Change, and Conversion*, ed. Robert Matthew Calhoun et al. (Mohr Siebeck, 2021), esp. 266–74.

14. Eusebius, *VC* 3.66, in *Eusebius: Life of Constantine*, trans. Averil Cameron and Stuart G. Hall, Clarendon Ancient History Series (Oxford University Press, 1999), 153. Cf. Michel-Yves Perrin, "*Crevit hypocrisis*: Limites d'adhésion au christianisme dans l'antiquité tardive: entre histoire et historiographie," in *Le problème de la christianisation du monde antique*, ed. Hervé Inglebert et al. (Picard, 2010). Perrin addresses Christians noticing other people's "interested" conversions.

15. Augustine, *Sermon* 62.7.

he was unsuited: his adult life had not been spent in the church he was being asked to lead. Though he was the son of a Christian mother, he made his way as a teacher of rhetoric, working first as a student, then with students, on the literary and grammatical aspects of traditional culture, including much classroom time spent discussing traditional, rather than Christian, myth. In time, Augustine frequented gatherings of the followers of Mani: Christians themselves, but well outside the bounds of what Augustine's mother would have imagined as Christian.

So, when Augustine was nudged to stand for election to bishop, his past was standing there with him, layers of life outside the church forming the backdrop against which he could be viewed. How could a year's worth of time spent preparing for the initiation be enough to change someone so quickly and also so thoroughly? The narrative of *Confessions* reframed that past, making Augustine's conversion into no change at all. In fact, with the right perspective, doubters could understand that he *had been* a sincere Christian, perhaps unwittingly but no less faithfully, *his entire life*. Though he had only joined up recently with the community he was going to lead, and though it seemed as if he had ignored the Christian discipline his mother had attempted to instill in him, instead preferring philosophy and rhetoric and eventually Manichaeism, Augustine had in fact been in conversation with—and had been wooed by!—the Christian god since his youth. This made his arrival among the Catholics into an inevitable disclosure of his true status; *Christian* was what he was beneath the surface, *always*, even as he tried on and tried out other communities for a time.[16] The thing is, one can hear the words a person says, check their correspondence with the words

---

16. Augustine does not invent this way of thinking about the inner essence; he just slots into it to his advantage. See also Jason BeDuhn, *Augustine's Manichaean Dilemma*, vol. 1, *Conversion and Apostasy, 373–388 C.E.* (University of

that were approved to be said, but ultimately words have the same problem as actions: they can be performed with or without sincerity and are thus unreliable indicators of a person's true (and perhaps hidden) nature or commitments. Augustine tries at length—eighty thousand words' worth—to make his real status and intentions known, even when his having performed the ritual of baptism *should* have been enough.[17]

To be a convert like Augustine was to some extent always to be on the docket for evaluation by others. In late ancient Christian literatures, there is the recurring desire to evaluate recent converts, to classify them as successfully and wholly turned from their prior lives, or not turned, and thus perhaps not fully Christian.[18] Writers across different communities marked the presence of half-Christians and sort-of Christians and false Christians, those who had in some way fulfilled the requirements for membership but drew the attention of their neighbors for having or seeming to have an incomplete commitment.[19] Converts were

---

Pennsylvania Press, 2009). See also the echoes of Justin's presentation of his past sampling in *Dialogue with Trypho* 2–3.

17. And of course, he was not actually a baptized Christian during that entire time; if he were, his mother would not have been working so hard to convert him.

18. Several modern writers note how relatively infrequently these labels appear, while they also make parallel arguments that there must have been more categorizing of this sort going on. See Charles Guignebert, "Les demi-chrétiens et leur place dans l'église antique," *Revue de l'histoire des religions* 88 (1923): 65–102, and Winfried Daut, "Die 'halben Christen' unter den Konvertiten und Gebildeten des 4. und 5. Jahrhunderts," *Zeitschrift für Missionswissenschaft und Religionswissenschaft* 55 (1971): 172–73. Interestingly, both of these are cited by Elizabeth G. Burr as if they do *not* hedge about how widespread the phenomenon is. See Burr, "Libanius of Antioch in Relation to Christians and Christianity: The Evidence of Selected Letters," *Topoi: Orient-Occident*, Supplément 7 (2006): 73n40.

19. Another on the list of scholarly studies of such Christians is Laurence Brottier, "Jean Chrysostome: un pasteur face à des demi-chrétiens," *Topoi* Suppl. 5 (2004): 439–57, esp. n. 10. See also Winrich A. Löhr, "Religious Truth,

under scrutiny in late antiquity and needed to make their loyalties visible in some way.[20] An eclectic selection of terms in the literature labels the incompletely converted: the semi-Christian, the demi-Christian, or, if you like it with a twinge of evaluation built in, the pseudo-Christian, or more taxonomic, the crypto-pagan or the crypto-Jew. That array represents the reality that Michel-Yves Perrin observed, which is that "ancient Christian discourse was marked by a veritable obsession about lying or passing which needed to be unmasked to get to the truth about behavior and being."[21] The impulse to identify, clarify, and classify aimed at knowledge, but the presence of so many labels points to the lack of knowledge, and more broadly, the insecurity of not knowing—and that itself is revealing.

II: WHAT LIES BENEATH

Ignorance can feel boundless, but it is not. In the mind, something known is constituted by a general size or shape, and then filled in with varying levels of detail, for more or less well-known parts; even what is not known has a shape. For instance, I know the city and county where I live very well. Because of how much I ride my bicycle through the area, I could be dropped

---

Dissimulation, and Deception in Late Antique Christianity" in *Double Standards in the Ancient and Medieval World*, ed. Karla Pollman (Duehrkohp & Radicke, 2000).

20. Béatrice Caseau, "Le crypto paganism et les frontières du licite: un jeu de masques?" in *Pagans and Christians in the Roman Empire: The Breaking of a Dialogue, (IVth–VIth Century A.D.)*, ed. Peter Brown and Rita Lizzi Testa (Lit, 2011).

21. *"Crevit hypocrisis,"* 20 (my translation): "Le discours chrétien antique est marqué par une véritable hantise de la dissimulation ou du travestissement qu'il s'agit de démasquer au profit de la vérité des comportements et des êtres." See also his n. 61, which provides an extensive bibliography of the issue.

randomly anywhere in about a thirty-mile radius of where I live and know exactly where I am and what is around me. My state, though, I know less well; I could identify my location in a few cities, but not in every mile on the grid of streets that fills most of Michigan. My region, the region around the Great Lakes, is even more sparsely represented in my imagination, huge pieces of it unrecognizable to me. But I do have a sense of its general shape, even if parts of it are entirely blank to me. The Great Lakes themselves are another story. Other than the thinnest outline of each—the shore where I have encountered their edges—I could not tell you a thing, could not even begin to represent the topography at their bottoms. And the bottom, too, is a kind of edge; think about the volume the water in each lake takes up. Lake Erie is shallow, an average of sixty-two feet deep, its bottom theoretically visible (were it not for the algae) from a boat anywhere on the surface. Lake Superior, though, is almost unfathomably deep—it contains enough water to cover every square mile of the Americas, North and South, to the depth of one foot. My ignorance of all Superior's contents is stark, but from its shoreline I at least know the general shape of what I do *not* know.

It is not only spatial ignorance that works this way but other kinds of ignorance too. Not knowing something leads to questioning, wondering, and then hypothesizing, accommodating, all of which are activities of projection, and that projection gives our lack of knowledge a structure. What we do not know, we can imagine, and the shape our imagination gives to the unknown will influence how we meet and use whatever information we subsequently gather about it. In the ancient world, and under imperial power, the peculiar shape of an ignorance could have the highest of stakes. For an example, I will go to the first century. Steven Weitzman has explained how the

Temple in Jerusalem was subject to both Roman power and the Roman gaze and thus was particularly vulnerable to invasion. Its interior, off limits to all outsiders and the vast majority of Jews, the site of ritual contact with the divine, was a kind of bait for hungry Roman eyes because it was unknown. So, Philo and Josephus attempted to curb the Roman will to know it by writing extravagantly of the Temple's exterior, lavishing their evocations with detail and luster, to draw the eye away from what could not be safely revealed and to satisfy it with seeing what could already be seen.[22] By morphing the external shape and nature of the Temple in their literary descriptions, these authors were attempting to control and redesign the shape of Roman ignorance, and with that shape, to control the impulse of Roman investigation.[23]

Unknown depths lie beneath the waves of Lake Superior, behind the façade of the Jerusalem Temple, and also, according to late ancient Christian thought, under the surface of the human being. Christians in late antiquity often made reference to formal concepts about the components of a human being, speaking of things like body and soul, or mind, or heart, or some combination thereof. Yet this kind of taxonomic psychology was not necessarily comprehensive; it did not govern all Christian thought about the human being. It may have dominated the formal treatises that discussed anthropology or the location of sin, or the ascetic advice that directed a person to discipline his impulses, but its

22. Steven P. Weitzman, *Surviving Sacrilege: Cultural Persistence in Jewish Antiquity* (Harvard University Press, 2005), chapter 4, "Optical Elusions."

23. See also Kim Bowes's exploration of the shape of indeterminate information in "Inventing Ascetic Space: Houses, Monasteries and the Archaeology of Asceticism," in *Western Monasticism ante litteram: The Spaces of Monastic Observance in Late Antiquity and the Early Middle Ages*, ed. Henrik Dey and Elizabeth Fentress (Brepols, 2011).

prevalence in these genres did not preclude Christians from conceptualizing the human being in other ways.

And conceptualize they did. Even the very same writers who employed the taxonomic terms of the soul and the passions that disturbed it, or the mind and the light that illumined it, could on occasion have a less technical, fuzzier concept of what the human being comprised. That alternate sense was not comprehensive, but interest- and domain-specific; it pops up where useful. In situations where Christians wondered about others' Christianness, people were imagined to be layered, duplex and possibly duplicitous, with a hidden substrate that could be the real thing, covered by some kind of surface that deceived.[24] That surface could be one's mien, one's words, one's actions, anything that could be ascertained by others; the substrate inside was not exactly interior, but it was by definition difficult to know or prove (in the testing sense). It was not visceral, exactly, though viscera could sometimes put it in evidence.[25]

Of course, being duplex implies the possibility of depth under the surface, and Christians wrote about evidence emerging from that depth in several ways. When Augustine spoke about the Christians who have the spirit of stubbornness inside them even after baptism, he also thought of their ongoing postbaptismal stubbornness coming out at some point in the future. "They may not show it, but then they go into labor and when the time comes they

---

24. This is literally the concept of insincerity, sincere being "without a wax layer."

25. Ellen Muehlberger, "The Legend of Arius's Death: Imagination, Space and Filth in Late Ancient Historiography," *Past & Present* 227 (2015): 3–29. See also David Frankfurter, *Evil Incarnate: Rumors of Demonic Conspiracy and Satanic Abuse in History* (Princeton University Press, 2006).

give birth to it."[26] A baby is evidence of many things: of a past act and of the processes inside the laboring mother, but it is in this metaphor the dark passenger who accompanies the baptized Christian. Their lack of Christianness will be known by that evidence once it passes to the outside. Or, left unbothered, it might remain inside.

That is the problem with a hidden interior: what it holds is not seen until it exits. Eusebius of Caesarea lamented fake Christians in explicitly architectural terms: there is "an unspeakable deceit" committed by "those who slipped into the church and adopted the false façade of the Christian name."[27] A Christian is herself a small building within the building of the church, containing herself behind a wall (or *schema*) that has been plastered onto her actual face, creating a façade. On one view, what is happening is that Christians are experiencing their ignorance of others, and then they express that suspicion by thinking in spatial terms. Yet the contours of the ignorance so imagined are important, because the peculiar shape assigned to the unknown can influence the inclinations that people have—both the amplitude of their desire to know and the methods they adopt for knowing.

A metaphor of a baby who reveals a truth to the world when born has obvious echoes in Christianity, while that of a person hiding behind a façade may seem like it has less potential to resonate. But structures matter in ancient Christianity—just not in the ways we might expect. Property was both salient in ancient Christian culture and consistently present in the enforcement of orthodoxy. When there are controversies over sectarian differences, heretical groups are denounced, but the teeth of the

---

26. *Enn. in Ps.* 34:9 (PL 36:328): "et si non exserunt, tamen parturiunt, et ubi locum inuenerint, pariunt."

27. Eusebius, *VC* 4.54.2, in *Eusebius: Life of Constantine*, trans, Averil Cameron and Stuart G. Hall (Oxford University Press, 1999), 174.

denunciations land on places, not people. A ruling given in 383 CE specified that "those vice-filled traditions which are detested by God and humanity . . . must not act as if they have the right to gather congregations or found churches in cities or fields or villages, with public or private funding."[28] The issuance went on to specify other restrictions, but its first order of business was to address the places—the buildings—that these groups might hold or build. Later laws were even more explicit about the centrality of buildings to the creation of orthodoxy. An issuance about heretical groups from 428 CE began with the requirement that it be "the highest priority that the churches they have stolen from the orthodox, wherever they may hold them, should be immediately handed over to the worldwide church."[29] The rest of the issuance dealt with other restrictions and punishments for heresy—heretics cannot ordain priests, they cannot reside in cities—but the very first matter, of "highest priority," was to assure that the properties heretics held were transferred to other Christians. Indeed, the right to transfer property—to leave a will or testament, to have heirs—was one of the main sites of governance and intervention against religious deviance. Those whose Christianness did not meet the standard were often barred from participating in the transactions that allowed transfers of property.[30] Not only is property a part of imperial designs for Christian conformity; it is central to the tradition's

28. *CTh* 16.5.12, in *Theodosiani libri XVI cum Constitutionibus Sirmondianis et Leges novellae ad Theodosianum pertinentes*, ed. Theodore Mommsen and Paul M. Meyer (Weidmanns, 1905), 1: 859–60 (my translation). Cf. *CTh* 16.1.3.

29. *CTh* 16.5.65 (*Theodosiani libri XVI*, 878–79, my translation). Cf. *CTh* 16.5.43.

30. *CTh* 16.5.23 revokes an earlier law that restricted inheritance rights; 16.5.40 specifies who can inherit a heretic; 16.8.7 directs a general confiscation for anyone who converts to Judaism.

expression and often appears first among the enforcements of its integrity.[31]

At first glance, to have this kind of focus on property could seem to be just a matter of what the empire could control; punitive measures tended to cluster around the rights granted to Roman citizens, because those were what could be taken away, and property holding and transfer were a substantial part of the portfolio of rights. The range of punishments *we* might envision, things like jail time or smaller fines, tended to not be used.[32] Property, though, held a special relationship with pious practice; they were entwined, one imagined to be necessary for the other. The extent of their pairing is visible in Eusebius's retelling of Constantine's efforts to support Christianity and quash other practices. As Eusebius spoke of the emperor's ban on pagan worship, consider just how that ban is effected:

> Next, two laws were simultaneously issued. One restricted the pollutions of idolatry which had for a long time been practised in every city and country district, so that no one should presume to set up cult-objects, or practise divination or other occult arts, or even to sacrifice at all. The other dealt with erecting buildings as places of worship and extending in breadth and length the churches of God, as if almost everybody would in future belong to God, once the obstacle of polytheistic madness had been removed.[33]

---

31. See also the letter of Constantine "to the East" preserved in Eusebius, *VC* 2.35–39, alongside the letter to Eusebius himself about restoring dilapidated churches at *VC* 2.4.6.

32. Although cf. Mark Letteney and Matthew D.C. Larsen, "A Roman Military Prison at Lambaesis," *Studies in Late Antiquity* 5.1 (2021): 65–102.

33. Eusebius, *VC* 2.45 (*Eusebius: Life of Constantine*, 110). See also *VC* 3.58: "Now however a fresh and chastening law was issued by the Emperor forbidding as criminal any of the old customs; for these persons also he provided written instructions, showing how he had been brought forward by God for this very purpose, of educating all mankind in laws of chastity; hence he did

Here, we see that activities—idolatry, divination, pagan sacrifice—were balanced by the creation not of opposing activities but of new properties. Of course, churches are where Christian activities take place, but it is important to grasp just how distinctive it is to locate this religious growth in a set of built structures.

It does not take much to see property and people as imbricated in this way because recent scholarship in early Christian studies has already explored how buildings are so much more than just structures. In addition to their physical presence as shelter, storage, and organizing architecture, buildings can influence and constrain the activity of human beings, so much so that we should consider this agency in studies of culture.[34] What is more, buildings can begin to blur into the very bodies of Christians. Kathryn Kleinkopf demonstrates how the habitations of ascetics, particularly those living in marginal circumstances, come to stand in as a part of themselves. The structure an ascetic chooses as a dwelling can become like a "second skin," Kleinkopf argues, so deeply representing the ascetic that its edifice can stand in for his face.[35] For Kleinkopf, the abode where a Christian dwells reveals and

---

not disdain to communicate even with them through a personal letter, and he urged them to turn earnestly to the knowledge of the Supreme. (3) There also he supported his words with matching actions, setting in their midst also a very large church building for worship, so that what had never yet from the beginning of time been heard of now became for the first time a fact . . ." (*Eusebius: Life of Constantine*, 146–47).

34. Catherine M. Chin, "Apostles and Aristocrats," in *Melania: Early Christianity through the Life of One Family*, ed. Catherine M. Chin and Caroline T. Schroeder (University of California Press, 2017), 20: "the creation of late ancient Christianity becomes a negotiation between human and non-human beings that lived on different timescales."

35. Kathryn Kleinkopf, "A Second Skin: Ascetics as Body-Places in Late Antique Christianity" (PhD diss., University of Tennessee, 2019). See especially the discussion at 31–32 and all of chapter 2, "The Physiognomy of the Landscape: Reading Place as Face."

transmits so much of that person that it was considered an inseparable part of that person while they resided there. They were a body-place, rather than a body inside a place.

What Kleinkopf has shown to be true in ascetic literature bears out in other Christian circumstances, particularly in the pursuit of knowledge about others. When Christians want to know about the Christianness of others whom they doubt, properties become an especially rich fund of information and eventually evidence to prove their deceit. Now, domestic houses in antiquity were in fact the site of all kinds of religious activity, both traditional and Christian.[36] And, traditional piety tended to localize in the main, accessible rooms of a house.[37] However, Kristina Sessa has documented a particular obsession for Christians: "the association of pagan rituals and objects with the *cubiculum*"—that is, the innermost, privatest room of a house—"appears to be a *topos* in Christian texts."[38] In several Roman martyr acts, pagans that come to be converted first reveal to Christians their stash of traditional objects—they come out of the *cubiculum*, a repository of secret things.[39] Where many scholars have seen in this topos the prospect of evidence of actual pagan practices,[40] I see the influence of the Christian way of prefiguring the unknown: proof of a person's

---

36. For Christians, see Kimberly Bowes, "Personal Devotions and Private Chapels," in *Late Ancient Christianity: A People's History of Christianity*, ed. Virginia Burrus (Fortress, 2005), 2:199–201.

37. See Kristina Sessa, "Christianity and the Cubiculum: Spiritual Politics and Domestic Space in Late Antique Rome," *Journal of Early Christian Studies* 15 (2007): 189n55.

38. Sessa, "Christianity and the Cubiculum," 188.

39. Sessa ("Christianity and the Cubiculum," 178) offers an overview of the illicit connotations of the *cubiculum*, which is "often cited as a site for the practice of magic and other illicit religious activities."

40. See the collection of scholarship on this sentiment listed by Sessa, "Christianity and the Cubiculum," 179–180n28.

duplicity is hidden deep in their properties, behind the façade the public could see.

What is true for individuals can be true for groups as well, as Christians also think of some public buildings as if they were people, filled with organic matter that can prove out. So, for instance, when Eusebius reflected on Constantine's practices, he visualized the actions taken against temples as disembowelments. In the *Life of Constantine*, he reported that pagans were finally convinced to leave behind their practices when they realized how vain they were. Their new sense of what was authentic piety and what was not came from the destruction of their buildings: "This was their inevitable reaction," Eusebius proclaimed, "when they saw hidden within the external form of the images a huge amount of foul matter." Temples were emptied to prove their vanity, because "inside were either bones and dry skulls from dead bodies which had been used for the devious magic arts of sorcerers, or foul rags full of disgusting filth, or a litter of hay and straw."[41]

What came out of temples was flesh and blood, but it was not healthy; decomposing, dry, rotted things existed behind the beauty one could normally see on the outside of the structure. In other references to the destruction of pagan temples, Eusebius made clear that the surface visible to most people was the thinnest of skins, a screen that just barely kept the "dark recesses" of temples from bursting forth to be known.[42] In some cases, the

41. VC 3.57 (*Eusebius: Life of Constantine*, 146).
42. VC 3.54 (*Eusebius: Life of Constantine*, 143–44): "Confident in the Emperor's piety and their own reverence for the Divinity, they visited populous communities and nations, and city by city, country by country, they exposed the long-standing error, ordering the consecrated officials themselves to bring out their gods with much mockery and contempt from their dark recesses into daylight, and then depriving them of their fine appearance and revealing to every eye the ugliness that lay within the superficially applied beauty."

contents of the despoiled temples were so foul that the emperor who uncovered it refused to show it to onlookers, in order to protect them.[43] Eusebius's perspective on these temples seemed to color later accounts of the same punitive actions. Rufinus, the writer who translated and extended Eusebius's *Church History*, followed the semantic pattern that Eusebius had established: he, too, reported on temples being filled with filthy things—"corpses and crimes" and "decapitated babies' heads" among them.[44] Other buildings can be filled with people and activity, but Christians saw pagan buildings filled with guts, carcasses, and rot, as if the temples themselves were corpses.

That is the discourse about how buildings provide proof of pious activity within. But evidentiary regimes tend to spread, and once buildings show that they *can* serve in this way, it is not long before they are called upon to show proof of what cannot otherwise be seen: their inhabitants' inclinations and intentions.

III: BREAKING IN

Thus, the pursuit of evidence can lead to other places, and here is a story from late antiquity that shows just how far some Christians would go.

Sometime near the turn from the fourth to the fifth century, a dispute sizzled between two men: one, a former governor of a province in Egypt, the other, the head of a couple monasteries

---

They then scraped off the material which seemed to be usable, purifying it by smelting with fire."

43. *VC* 3.55.4.

44. Rufinus, *Church History* 11.24, in *The Church History of Rufinus of Aquileia, Books 10 and 11*, trans. Philip R. Amidon (Oxford University Press, 1997), 83.

near the town where that man lived. The former governor, named Gesios, had come to seem suspicious to the head of the monasteries, Shenoute. Gesios had attended Shenoute's sermons, had pledged money to Shenoute's enterprises, and had even said that he was interested in the rituals that might have marked his entry into the church. In other words, Gesios showed all the right signs. Shenoute, though, increasingly suspected all this to be false, and broke into the governor's house, twice, to prove it. He had made complaints about Gesios's misuse of his wealth, as well as his mistreatment of his workers and the poor in general, but once inside the house, Shenoute did not take money or valuable items. Instead, he searched, penetrating to the recesses of the house to find what he had become convinced he would find: evidence of Gesios's duplicity—namely, objects (Shenoute thought of them as idols) that showed Gesios retained some practices Shenoute thought he should reject.

Breaking into this man's house, twice, was not the most violent thing Shenoute had ever done. From other writings by him and about him, we hear that he punched the heretic Nestorius at the Council of Ephesus; he executed a scissor hold on a government official who came to his monastery; he used forms of corporal punishment on his monks that sound extreme, considering them a necessary form of discipline (as Rebecca Krawiec has astutely argued).[45] Violence was a sure feature of Shenoute's interactions with those under his control and on his turf. The entry to Gesios's house was a little different: here, he was entering a home, not attacking a person. But he justified the break-in with a framework supporting a much more disturbing violence. Scripture

---

45. Rebecca Krawiec, *Shenoute and the Women of the White Monastery: Egyptian Monasticism in Late Antiquity* (Oxford University Press, 2002).

authorized his actions, he argued, in a text written sometime after 395 CE:

> Let our eyes—in accordance with the scriptures—look at what is right, and let our eyelids gaze at just things, and we will recognize how great is the impurity of the soul of every pestilential person who is inimical toward the faith of the universal Church. For not only does the great prophet Moses command, "Be not lawless," and, "Make no graven images for yourselves in the likeness of any image, *etc*... and, "Lift not your eyes up to heaven and see the sun and the moon and the stars and all the order of heaven and go astray and worship them and serve them," but he also ordered, "If they set them up, they will be killed."[46]

These are the words of a man who understands his actions are under question, but also of a man who imagines that he has a flawless defense in scripture. To Shenoute, Christians can—and in fact, *should*—gaze upon others, glimpse into their souls, and stand ready to punish them with death.

This is the shape of aspirational Christian power in late ancient Egypt. Shenoute imagined that entering Gesios's house would give him proof of what he already knew, in part because built places are intertwined with people in his thought. In that same sermon, *Let Our Eyes*, Shenoute explained how the hearts of non-Christians could be a habitation for demons:

> The birds that fly in the air also have their nests on the tips of tree branches, but more often in desert places. For their part, the nests of the spirits of wickedness are the hearts of every pagan and every heretic, who are like deserts because there is neither faith nor fear

---

46. Shenoute, *Let Our Eyes*, trans. and ed. Stephen Emmel, in *Selected Discourses of Shenoute the Great: Community, Theology, and Social Conflict in Late Antique Egypt*, ed. David Brakke and Andrew Crislip (Cambridge University Press, 2015), 206.

of God in them. These are the places about which the prophets spoke, saying, "The demons will dance there." For when serpents grow weak from being stabbed inside of crevices, they can still spit out water at their attackers. Just so, when the unclean spirits grow weak from being stabbed with their attackers' faith and their love for Jesus, they can do nothing as they writhe from side to side except spit out lies and insults through the mouths of those whose hearts serve them as nests when they come to be enclosed inside them since they are also pursued in the air when true Christians spread out their hands.[47]

This can seem metaphorical—demons are "in the hearts" of pagans and heretics—but from Shenoute's exposition, we can see that this was no metaphor. This was really happening! Shenoute had a theory about why demons would take up residence in persons. He explained that they are then sheltered from the danger that Christians pose for them when they reside simply in the air. When the demons are attacked in their human shelters, like snakes when they are attacked though they hide in crags, demons show signs of distress—namely, the lies and insults that come from the mouths of those they inhabit. Real insults, real mouths, real perils in the air—demons do not *sort of* nest in people. They nest in people.

At the same time, houses are also habitual lodgings for demons, containing them and the paraphernalia they require. In a short speech Shenoute gave to the people who supported Gesios, he compares the things that happen to pious people, his people, with what happens to wicked people—that is, Gesios's people. "The house of God [is] the Church," he wrote, "which illumines the entire earth and is filled with words of life, but as for their houses, which have

---

47. Shenoute, *Let Our Eyes*, 207. Compare his description of two-hearted people (those who were not committed enough to Christianity for his taste) in *As I Sat on a Mountain*.

become lodgings for the demons and are filled with deceitful books and every false thing, they are ruined in them."[48] The houses of Gesios and the people with him are exactly like their hearts: the lodging of demons. As you can see, this framework—"home is where the heart is"—is less a metaphor than an anthropological concept. We know that Christians had a broad range of concepts of the person and the body, and I would add this to the list. Shenoute imagines people and their built environments as part of the same entity, their acts and their homes to be one.

The equation powers other screeds, such as in *God Is Blessed*, where Shenoute railed against people who participated in "unnatural" sexual acts. His suggestion was that they be robbed, stripped, "their houses plundered by the enemy," as these people "recline in evil," "they sleep in unnatural acts," as if their actions were their beds. They reside in their houses *and* inside their sins, resting there as if in a private chamber (the very kind of chamber where their sins bloom!). This much accords with what scholars have argued about his concept of his own monastery—a building, a compound, but also an organic entity that could hold and pass sin.[49] Shenoute knew the world through a frame of thinking that morphs built environment into a body, and more than that, into a person, such that the interior of a house, in its solitude and its boundedness from the world, can hold the promise of containing something that is there to be known, something tangible to be revealed about its inhabitant.

48. Shenoute, *God Says Through Those Who Are His*, trans. and ed. Stephen Emmel, in Brakke and Crislip, *Selected Discourses*, 274.
49. Drawing on the sermon *God Is Holy* and other pieces from Shenoute's *Canon* 7, Caroline T. Schroeder paralleled the building of the White Monastery and the holiness of the monks in it, overwritten with the holiness of Christ's body. See Schroeder, *Monastic Bodies: Discipline and Salvation in Shenoute of Atripe* (University of Pennsylvania Press, 2007).

Houses, then, hold the key for proving what Christians already know, and that is why a house is at the center of Shenoute's campaign against Gesios. And it *is* a campaign, taking place over multiple encounters and with Shenoute always taking the aggressor's role. It is clear that some—Gesios, at least, and perhaps other villagers—thought of Shenoute as a robber, but the monk had a different view. Famously, he argued:

> For just as there is no "robbery" for those who truly have Jesus—with respect to what you have said about me because I took your gods secretly and because I caused your disgrace and shame to be attached to the doorposts of your house, written on sheets of papyrus, after your jars of urine, bottled as if it were wine, were broken upon the steps of your house and into your doorway and the door of those who resemble you—(so too) there is no "freedom" for those who put their trust in Kronos, namely, you and those who imitate you in acts of disbelief and all uncleanness.[50]

The crime, or noncrime, under discussion is much more than just a home invasion. Shenoute sent letters, posted flyers, brought and broke jars of wine (or urine, or wine so bad it might as well be urine?). And then he broke in.

The actual breaking and entering is also something we know about because Shenoute described it, too. He demurred about what he was being charged with by others, but in apologizing to some villages, he revealed the details of what he had done:

> They lied about me in the house of a blasphemer against Jesus because I took his gods, whom he worships by lighting a lot of lamps for them, and offering up incense to them on the altars with what is called kuphi, and breaking bread before them. And because we

---

50. Shenoute, *Not Because a Fox Barks*, in Brakke and Crislip, *Selected Discourses*, 201.

made an example of him by removing his idols from a private chamber during the night quietly even though the doors protected them securely.[51]

Shenoute entered Gesios's house and, through divine assistance, arrived at its very center to reveal the things that proved Gesios to be false. At his will, the house coughed up the evidence of what Gesios attempted to hide, and what Shenoute had known all along.

The documents around Gesios's case make clear that Shenoute had done the same on at least two other occasions: taking what he thought were idols and some books, and killing several household animals, which he assumed must have been meant for eventual sacrifice. In each case, the building associated with Gesios contained what was available to be known, a framing that more than justifies—indeed, necessitates—unwanted entry to the house in question. It is this kind of conceptualization—the imagined structure that enables, or requires, violent entry—that draws my attention. It could be dismissed as idiosyncratic, merely Egyptian or Shenoutean, if it were not the driving force behind a second story.

IV: THE PICTURE OF PIETY

The second story of breaking and entering comes from a different time and place, yet it too depends on houses to be the proof of

51. Shenoute, *Let Our Eyes*, 209. The text continues: "He (Jesus) who brought his fear upon those living there and around there . . . was also the one who enabled us to open the doors as he wanted. It was also he who led us through the atrium and up the stairway of that house until we came upon those abominations although they were hidden away. And it was he who made straight our entry and our exit. And it was through him that we exposed them (the abominations) openly so as for everyone to recognize his (Gesios') contempt and his shame, for them to recognize that he is a liar for having said, 'There are no idols in my house,' when I asked him, since Jesus, in whom he does not believe, has exposed his moral failings."

a person's piety, or the lack thereof. The *Church History* by John of Ephesus, composed in the sixth century, includes a concatenation of stories that illumine the themes of houses as repositories of evidence for persons, Christian vigilance and neglect regarding others' religious practice, and the duplicity of those who pretend to be Christian. The chain starts with a report that a group of Satan worshippers at Heliopolis were intent upon doing the local Christians harm.[52] Many of these "heathen" were arrested and tortured until they gave up the names of the others in their network; violence against them brought out the identities of other members of the group when no other method was working. The authorities approached the house of one Rufinus, living at Antioch, who had been named in this process. He was not there, so they traveled to his house in Edessa and found an actual sacrifice to Zeus taking place, Rufinus in the middle of it all.

The ostensible purpose of the raid had been fulfilled—Rufinus had been found, his deviance confirmed—but the house was brimming with more information to spill. Most of the others gathered at his house ran away, but as John of Ephesus told it, Rufinus knew he was caught. "Knowing well that he had no place of refuge to which he could escape," Rufinus "drew his knife, and smote it into his heart, and having given himself a wound in the abdomen, fell down dead. There was, however, a gouty old man, too feeble to flee, and an old woman, whom on entering they found still present, with the dying body of Rufinus stretched upon the ground, and surrounded by the preparations for sacrifice." The prime target, Rufinus, was able to get away, after a fashion, by taking his own life. The house, though, bore evidence against him on the inside, its contents giving proof of what he was. Remaining

52. John of Ephesus, *Church History* 3.27, in *The Third Part of the Ecclesiastical History of John Bishop of Ephesus*, trans. R. Payne Smith (Oxford University Press, 1860), 209.

members,⁵³ barely alive, feeble and perhaps fetid, fan out alongside his own body like the victims of the sacrifice, a tableau of falsity. And in one way of thinking, they are indeed victims, and they are at the same time the viscera of this body-house, whose presence speaks to what kind of person Rufinus really was, on the inside. The searchers may have found its inhabitant dead, but his house was alive—maybe just barely so, but enough to render a confession of sorts.

Then, confessions gotten by violence added more links to the chain of evidence. The two elderly participants were tortured for information. As John narrated:

> Upon them they laid hands, and threatened them with instant death, unless they truly declared the names of all who had taken part in these proceedings; but if they would make a full confession, they promised that no harm should happen to them. And they being in terror of death, told all their names, and among them was the governor and procurator, Anatolius.⁵⁴

In addition to the gory exhibit of the bodies, there were these two witnesses who were pressed for information. Still alive, and most importantly, still there to give testimony, to keep the trail hot, identifying yet another heathen to track down—namely, Anatolius.

Anatolius's story is the next link in the chain. Leaving Rufinus's house behind, the crowd went after him, and as they pursued him, he attempted to disguise his real whereabouts, with little effect.⁵⁵ In the breach, Anatolius's house gave him away in the most spectacular manner. John narrated the practically miraculous outing:

---

53. Cf. the echo of this man and woman as evidence in *Church History* 3.31.
54. John of Ephesus, *Church History* 3.28 (*Third Part*, 210–11).
55. John of Ephesus, *Church History* 3.28 (*Third Part*, 211–13).

As for Anatolius, having set up in his house a picture of our Lord, in the hope of making people erroneously suppose that he was a Christian, he invited a number of persons to come and see it. But as he was shewing it, the picture turned hindside foremost with its face to the wall, so that astonishment fell upon all who witnessed it. Anatolius, however, turned it back again, and put it right; but suddenly, a second time, it turned round; and again a third time. And upon this they examined it closely, and found skillfully introduced into the back a likeness of Apollo so carefully done as not to be visible without looking closely at it. Horrified at the sight, the archers threw him on the ground, and kicked him, and dragged him by the hair to the Praetorium, where they declared all that had happened: and, as was said, finding escape impossible, he also made a full deposition of every thing.[56]

The picture was a subterfuge, the face of Jesus set out by Anatolius as camouflage for his real pieties. As if it sensed the visitors, it took on a life of its own, turning its obverse again and again to out Anatolius as perverse. He tried to fight the picture, but the picture won because it drew the close attention of the visitors and, under examination, revealed its true nature: no portrait of Christ but a picture of Apollo. Even though it is fainter, even though it is on the back of a painting, even though it is decidedly *not* what Anatolius wanted to display for others to see, it was visible on inspection and gave him away. Walls in this case did not make the Christian, but they certainly did break him; the portrait of Apollo/Jesus had been waiting there on the wall to tell its story, to make its turn, to do the big reveal, to accuse Anatolius.

And yet, to do that work, the portrait required people who could look at it, who were willing to examine it, as the image of Apollo was not visible without careful scrutiny. There is a

---

56. John of Ephesus, *Church History* 3.29 (*Third Part*, 214).

significant tension in late ancient texts about the value of invasiveness in cases of scandal—just how closely should those in the majority look to find deviance in their midst? On the one hand, there is an attitude of restraint, captured for example in the *Theodosian Code*. This imperial legal anthology is a kind of snapshot of what was happening, or what emperors hoped would happen, in the realm of social standards, expectations, and enforcement. Caroline Humfress has detailed the relative restraint on hand in the code, where invasion into pagan property is limited.[57] But it also records just how hard it was to get people to think about invasiveness, to get them to participate in seeking out information about their neighbors, or even to get people to think of religion as something that needed regulation in the first place and, if violated, required punishment.

On the other hand, there are stories like these from John of Ephesus's *Church History*, in which officials never look quite hard enough for deviance, so everyday Christians have to make the effort to reveal the heathens. Where kings and magistrates were neglectful, crowds of Christians were vigilant. Such is the case in Placidia, where

> while there were known to be in the city many followers of heathenism, the people considered that the court acquitted whom they chose, such, that is, as gave money, and whom they chose they unjustly condemned; and that the quest for the heathen was carelessly and corruptly carried on: and the more so as the king was indifferent to it, and had gone out to one of his country palaces, and what was done was kept secret from all eyes.[58]

---

57. Caroline Humfress, "Law in Practice," in *A Companion to Late Antiquity*, ed. Philip Rousseau (Blackwell, 2009), 377–91.

58. John of Ephesus, *Church History* 3.30 (*Third Part*, 215).

The people know about the system and demand that it work differently. They "began suddenly to gather in the heart of the city" in large crowds, chanting "'Out with the bones of the dicasts!' 'Out with the bones of the heathens!'"[59] What the magistrates shy away from, what the bishop refuses, the crowd was eager to do.

The telling of the story makes clear that the purpose of the crowd was not desire, or greed, but knowledge. At one point, they come across a horde of gold during their housebreaking, and the official with them tried to get them to take it, to give up, and to go away. That is when they protest, "as with one mouth, the whole multitude called out, 'We are no thieves: we are Christians, and assembled in Christ's cause, to avenge the wrongs of Christianity upon the heathen. Keep your gold for yourself; we touch it not.'"[60] The crowd was not interested in the things of exchange value in these houses; money did not mean a thing to them. The real value is the epistemological certainty on offer from *other* objects in the house. There is a gradient of value, and those contents that have the most monetary value are comparatively worthless when it comes to signaling the commitment of a person to Christianity. The search for the most valuable evidence takes Christians all the way into other people's spaces, their homes ransacked not for profit but for proof.

CONCLUSION: ACCESSING THE HIDDEN TRUTH

The exercise of power in late antiquity took many forms. There is power over the bodies of others, held by male heads of households;

---

59. John of Ephesus, *Church History* 3.31 (*Third Part*, 216).

60. A second time a crowd presses an official to take the threat seriously, almost violently. Finally, they extract a promise from him. He says, "'make no tumult, but return to the city, and we will immediately return there ourselves, and do what you wish; nor will we neglect the matter'" (John of Ephesus, *Church History* 3.31 [*Third Part*, 220]).

there is the power to rule, to make licit and illicit, to respond with soldiers, held by emperors; there is the power to exploit, financially or physically, held by the rich; there is the power to shame, held by the pious. And in addition to being *multi*valent, power in late antiquity was *ambivalent*: fortunes rose and fell, people came into power and lost it. That ambivalence is especially present within Christianity. The shifting imperial favor for one group of Christians over another, the messy exercise of trying to figure out a consensus and enforce it—these things *moved* in late antiquity. Power under construction like this can seem capricious, to observers and to its subjects. It is power under construction, then, that is most likely to generate justifications of its exercise.

Such justifications can reveal how that power is exercised, and along what lines it will be distributed. Often, justifications are analogical frames: the situation under scrutiny is *just like* this other situation, so the flow of power should proceed the same. Through such frames, encounters with power are shot through with imagined elements. Recently, in the *Journal of Early Christian Studies*, Carly Daniel-Hughes and Maia Kotrosits explained how this worked in the writings of a much earlier writer, the third-century Christian author Tertullian. Scenes he wrote have often been taken as documentary, a record of Christian encounters with Roman law, but Kotrosits and Daniel-Hughes demonstrate that there is a significant portion of Tertullian's accounts that are, in their phrasing, "juridical fantasies."[61] In these imagined scenes, Christians like Tertullian fantasized about being put through the paces, and thus being known, by a legal system that did not, as best as we can see, actually pay them much mind.

61. Maia Kotrosits and Carly Daniel-Hughes, "Tertullian of Carthage and the Fantasy Life of Power: On Martyrs, Christians, and Other Attachments to Juridical Scenes," *Journal of Early Christian Studies* 28 (2020): 1–31.

Christian power, framed in later antiquity, looks a lot like these juridical fantasies, but in reverse. It is not about being under scrutiny oneself, but about calling *others* to account, putting *others* through their paces, knowing them, in the most indicative cases, better than they know themselves. The process assumes a duplex subject, if not a duplicitous one: there is what you can know about yourself, and there is what *I* can see, and that is always more. How could one possibly prove it, though? Disease or death, the organic processes of the body that God was assumed to have created and that he still controlled as a part of the natural world, were perceived to be sure signs. A terrible end could reveal what had been true all along, the persistent resident evil in a person that had escaped notice.[62] If disease or death did not come quickly enough for the proving, there was always the bank of evidence stashed away in a person's dwelling, their building and its contents giving a foundation to Christian knowledge.

The information gathering that Christians do in these cases, then, is in a sense apocalyptic. The purpose of the evidence gathered is not to unveil truly new things, nor is it aimed at the discovery of novel perspectives. Instead, evidence is found when it is needed to corroborate a truth already known. Thus, much of Christian history-making is a matter of drawing the physical world into a state that will offer proof of what is in the imagination, either by creating things in the physical world, like sites or buildings or relics or documents, or by repurposing those

---

62. See my chapter on awful death in *Moment of Reckoning: Imagined Death and Its Consequences in Late Ancient Christianity* (Oxford University Press, 2019); Jennifer Barry, *Bishops in Flight* (University of California Press, 2019), esp. chapter 4, "To Rehabilitate and Return a Bishop in Flight," 103–30. See also the very common disease language use for heresy, as in Cyril of Alexandria, *First Letter to Succensus*, 2–3, in *Cyril of Alexandria: Select Letters*, ed. and trans. Lionel R. Wickham (Clarendon, 1983), 71, 73.

things that already exist, framing them anew to become the substantiation of Christian inklings about others.[63] Elsewhere, I have termed this general tendency to be Christianity's project of "perpetual adjustment," producing evidence from many sources to validate the changing knowledge of what has happened in the past. When giving attestation is so prioritized, finding evidence is a necessity, so it can take place by any means. As Shenoute observed, there is no crime in robbery "for those who have Jesus," just as in John of Ephesus's *Church History* the crowd says they are not there to be robbers; instead, they are Christian. In both retorts, the license for violently executed scrutiny is directly tied to Christian identity. The evaluation of religious deviance is inseparable from this license. Violence then can produce the proof it seeks, recasting the world according to the Christian knower: a seemingly Christian neighbor can be semi-Christian, insufficiently Christian, even falsely Christian, and eventually be found out.

---

63. The landscape (or the natural world or the created world and everything in it) keeps the score. For other Christian interactions with hidden things, see Caseau, "Le crypto paganisme"; David Frankfurter, *Christianizing Egypt: Syncretism and Local Worlds in Late Antiquity* (Princeton University Press, 2018).

CHAPTER THREE

The Advent of the Superfather

The story of early Christianity can be told many ways, but it is often related as a series of achievements. After the decriminalization of Christian practice in the early fourth century, Christian communities grew in number and power, beginning the journey toward a consensus that would span both space and time. Disagreements, when they were disruptive enough, were handled at conferences called by, and funded by, interested emperors, and at them, learned bishops could hash out new articulations of their truths on God, or clarify difficult variations in practice. In this story, the largest, most important conferences—labeled "ecumenical councils" because they seemed to bring together the *oikumene*, the whole inhabited world—appear on the timeline of the early church like a string of oases in the desert, places arrived at with difficulty but also places to rest assured: the Council of Nicaea in 325 CE, the Council of Constantinople in 381 CE, of Ephesus in 431 CE, and of Chalcedon in 451 CE. Because of the importance that the later tradition accorded these four councils, they are significant in the study of Christianity; and because they are occasions of men making decisions, of church and state convening, occasions of public declarations preserved with political and social consequences to follow, they have intrigued historians looking at the ancient world. For their salience, ecumenical councils seem like a historian's dream, as they appear to offer clarity in a landscape of complexity.[1]

The names of the first four ecumenical councils—Nicaea, Constantinople, Ephesus, Chalcedon—have worked like little oases for newcomers to the study of Christianity in late antiquity, too. Patristic theology is complex enough to sustain a lifetime of study, but students have to start somewhere. Whatever else happened at these councils (and a lot else did), newcomers can enter by learning that at Nicaea, the status of Christ as the Son was codified; at Constantinople, assertions about the Son's nature were extended to the Holy Spirit; at Ephesus, the nature of Christ's human mother was established; and at Chalcedon, the community agreed on Christ's own nature (or natures). As students continue to read about the development of early Christian thought, they come to see the variation and nuance represented in each meeting, the agreements or disagreements that each one inaugurated or solidified. And yet, the field they are exploring as they read is structured, on a basic level, by these councils. There are collections of ancient Christian writings divided into ante-Nicene, Nicene, and post-Nicene eras; Christological developments are marked by their relation to either the Council of Ephesus or the Council of Chalcedon; even groups of Christians are labeled "Chalcedonian" or "anti-Chalcedonian" as a kind of

---

1. Even the creation of collected anthologies titled "Acts" to represent their proceedings is an activity aimed at displaying unity and control. See Thomas Graumann, *The Acts of the Early Church Councils: Production and Character*, Oxford Early Christian Studies (Oxford University Press, 2021).

marker of allegiance. In their own time, councils produced as many problems as solutions, but for the modern study of ancient Christianity, they simplify, helping students and scholars organize their knowledge.

The Second Council of Constantinople should, for many reasons, enjoy the same importance and familiarity as its predecessors. It took place in 553 CE, just a century after the Council of Chalcedon, and it was convened when an energetic, interventionist emperor with long-standing theological interests called together more than one hundred and fifty bishops to a major city. Over the course of a month, the group debated the significance of past theological positions. At the end, the large majority of those present signed the council's conclusions, which then became widely influential. What is more, this fifth ecumenical council has left behind an "exceptionally rich" archive; while its acts in the original Greek do not survive, two ancient Latin translations do, and they show us extensive transcripts created for all the sessions, including what was read, what was said, and who agreed, with copies of other documents important for the discussion appended.[2] For these reasons, when compared with the first four councils, the Second Council of Constantinople should be at least as salient as they are, and in fact, it could be considered an even *more* promising event for study by historians.

And yet, it has been discounted, left to linger as a barely remembered tagalong to the first four. Perhaps that is because it occurs so

2. Richard Price, ed. and trans., *The Acts of the Council of Constantinople of 553, with Related Texts on the Three Chapters Controversy*, 2 vols., Translated Texts for Historians 51 (Liverpool University Press, 2009), 1:viii. See 1:104–8 for a detailed description of the production and reception of the *Acts* in antiquity. Price compiles the attendees and signatories in 2:287–99; 168 bishops were present in the city for the council, with 152 listed in the Acts as attending and sixteen others gathered elsewhere in protest.

deep into late antiquity. The study of early Christianity often nestles itself within the study of the Roman Empire, and by 553 that empire was, according to the historical consensus, fallen. Or perhaps it is because of the challenges of understanding the various communities in conflict at the Second Council of Constantinople. Many histories of early Christianity end at the Council of Chalcedon in 451—beyond that point, Christianity is a bit unwieldy, as the community divides theologically and linguistically, with key texts now not just in Greek and Latin but also in Syriac and Coptic. It may be that the history after Chalcedon is just too Byzantine, literally and figuratively. Then again, the council's relative obscurity could just be a cognitive tic: it may be that the Second Council of Constantinople is discounted because it is *second*—that is, it is the city's second time hosting an important council, which disrupts that more manageable mnemonic of Nicaea, Constantinople, Ephesus, Chalcedon.

More than just discounted, the Second Council of Constantinople is lamented. Richard Price has recently produced an English translation of the *Acts* from the council, and by way of introduction, he surveyed the council's reception among modern readers. It fared badly with two different audiences. Those looking back at the Second Council of Constantinople from within Christian tradition disparage it, Price reports, as they find "its decrees regrettable and its methods deplorable."[3] Those who study the council from a historical perspective share the sentiment, as Price recounts that scholarship has found it to be "by far the most problematic of all the councils."[4] The council's purpose was to evaluate the

3. Price, *Acts of Constantinople*, 1:vii.
4. Price, *Acts of Constantinople*, 1:vii, citing Wilhelm De Vries, *Orient et Occident: les structures ecclésiales vues dans l'histoire des sept premiers conciles oecuméniques* (Éditions du Cerf, 1974), 161.

works and person of Theodore of Mopsuestia, some writings by Theodoret of Cyrrhus, and a letter attributed to Ibas of Edessa—all of which were tagged together as "The Three Chapters." Price reports that over the course of the council participants used "brutality toward ... opponents," "falsification of documents," and the "doubtful procedure of posthumous condemnation," as the discussions "plumbed at times the depth of misplaced ingenuity."[5] An expert in church history, in a project aimed at reviving historical interest in the Second Council of Constantinople, he could not help but label it a "bizarre drama."[6] And Price was not wrong; the council *was* a drama. Even as participants attempted to square the strictures of tradition and authority with correct belief—as this Christian community tried to define "its identity by mapping and interpreting its past"—they also engaged in several innovative strategies.[7] The resulting oddities included judging the dead and falsely declaring to be forgeries texts previously affirmed as authentic, things difficult to compute alongside the rubric of the earlier four councils.

These oddities, the very things that have given the Second Council of Constantinople its regrettable reputation, are also evidence that it was the site of something new emerging in early Christian culture. Deposited in the record from the council are indications of a happening of, if not exactly theological, then at least superhuman proportions. It has gone unrecognized because, unlike the developments at previous ecumenical councils, what was emerging at Constantinople in 553 was not explicitly discussed. There was no creed produced to detail this new concept, no testimony to outline what had become the consensus

5. Price, *Acts of Constantinople*, 1:viii.
6. Price, *Acts of Constantinople*, 1:51.
7. Price, *Acts of Constantinople*, 1:viii.

position. What happened is visible in the way the council wobbles away from the patterns of its predecessors. Acting a bit like an object on a trajectory near a much more massive, though unseen, object, the council deviated from the norm in both literary practices and historical perspectives.

Its deviation indicates the presence of something immense. While late ancient Christian culture already revered authors of the past as special and authoritative, these "fathers of the church" were transcended at the Second Council of Constantinople by an even stronger entity: the superfather. Not a human being or a god, the superfather is a transtemporal guarantor of orthodoxy. He is without will or substance, existing as a dossier, but not necessarily linked to specific utterances or passages. In what follows, I will first explain how the culture of the fathers of the church created the conditions for a superfather to emerge. Neither necessary nor foreseen, this new kind of being came into existence as the result of an accident, I argue; I will then describe how the odd actions taken at the Second Council of Constantinople confirm the existence of the new being.

We will see along the way that the tools that historians have used so far to parse what happened at the council have been inadequate, because they were miscalibrated for what they were attempting to register. With a different lens in hand, we see that the oddities become more comprehensible, more predictable; they become sources of evidence instead of anomalies to be brushed away. The council was, among other things, the advent of the superfather, and thus it was as generative, as important in Christian culture, as any other ecumenical council before it. That is because the emergence of the superfather is also key to understanding how we see Christianity *now*, as expectations about him shaped processes of collection and transmission, the very making of the early Christian author, and thus the archive by which we access the early Christian past.

I: THE FORCE OF THE FATHER

Late ancient Christian knowledge of the divine was the result of a robust, constructive enterprise, taken on by writers who sought to articulate, as best they could, concepts that were at heart mysterious. On the agenda in the fourth and fifth centuries were issues like the precise details of the engendering of a cosmic being that existed simultaneously both in time and outside of time; the mechanism by which this being's death—both final and reversible—changed the status of every member of the human species; the existence of a separate, but somehow identical, entity that was one with it, yet appeared in different forms and at different events in time; or the medical logic and reproductive processes that allowed a woman to bear the being with her human body. All of these required extraordinary thought and effort. If they are familiar or the challenges they pose seem unremarkable, take it as a sign of how thoroughly such Christian theological concepts have been dispersed in societies where Christianity dominated (I have listed here the topics of the Trinitarian and Nestorian controversies, those conversations that solidified at the Council of Nicaea, the First Council of Constantinople, and the Council Ephesus).

However familiar they may or may not be now, these concepts were deeply strange in antiquity. By that I mean simply that they were not obvious or commonsensical; nor were they aligned with any erudite philosophical precept of the time. Their parameters were not to be found immediately in the books that Christians revered as scripture, and what proof could be brought forward from narrative scenes or dialogue in that scripture was not self-evident as such. That is to say, the construction of even a temporary consensus around any one of these topics—let alone all of them—was an achievement reached by extensive, long-term, focused intellectual effort.

Helping considerably were the writings of earlier men, compatriots engaged in the same project, even if decades or centuries prior. Late ancient Christians aiming at theological clarity brought the riches of older writing into their own prose. At first they followed the citational habits of the traditions around them—namely, by not really citing at all. Ancient writers, Christian writers among them, often took good ideas or formulations and brought their gist and sometimes their verbatim expression into their own writing without indication of the source, a process Mark Vessey has described as a "silent assimilation."[8] Though it may seem like a bad thing, this practice was usually seen by ancient people as evidence of their respect for tradition; a correct concept would not belong to a single person. Having access to an earlier man's work on a topic, or even as a prolegomenon to thinking about a topic, powered writers through the challenges of their own day; leaving earlier contributions unmarked helped new writing align with traditions of old.

Over time, in antiquity a different practice took hold among Christians. Writers in the later fourth century began to tag good ideas and adept formulations with the names of their authors, particularly in theological discussions. This was in part the result of Christians developing a finer sense of a canon of their tradition's past literature, complete with the implied debt new writers should pay to their predecessors, as might happen with

---

8. Mark Vessey, "The Forging of Orthodoxy in Latin Christian Literature: A Case Study," *Journal of Early Christian Studies* 4 (1996): 495–513, at 501.

any textual community. Scholars have identified the practice in early Christian writers across geographic regions and linguistic communities, from Augustine of Hippo to Severus of Antioch.[9] Christians located esteemed authors in the past, used their thought *and* brought them into present conversations, by name or even with simply the generic label "father," a change that Vessey identifies as nothing short of "a revolution in Christian literary practice."[10] That revolution extended beyond literature into the very sense that Christians had of themselves as a community. As the practice marked individual authors from the past, at the same time it built up an idea that there were a collective of "fathers" from the past who required attention and allegiance. Thomas Graumann has documented the long-term change in how Christian writers spoke of themselves—a shift toward referring not just to the church and its traditions but to the church of the fathers, a community that aligned the living with the most important men of the past and that, most importantly, was then beholden to their example in thought and practice.[11]

---

9. Éric Rebillard, "A New Style of Argument in Christian Polemic: Augustine and the Use of Patristic Citations," *Journal of Early Christian Studies* 8 (2000): 559–78. See also Yonatan Moss, "'Packed with Patristic Testimonies': Severus of Antioch and the Reinvention of the Church Fathers," in *Between Personal and Institutional Religion: Self, Doctrine, and Practice in Late Antique Eastern Christianity*, ed. Brouria Bitton-Ashkelony and Lorenzo Perrone, CELAMA 15 (Brepols, 2013), 227–50. Susanna Elm identifies Gregory of Nazianzus as one who is turned into a "father" in "A Programmatic Life: Gregory of Nazianzus' *Orations* 42 and 43 and the Constantinopolitan Elites," *Arethusa* 33 (2000): 411–27.

10. Vessey, "Forging of Orthodoxy," 499–500.

11. Thomas Graumann, *Die Kirche der Väter: Vätertheologie und Väterbeweis in den Kirchen des Ostens bis zum Konzil von Ephesus (431)*, Beiträge zur historischen Theologie 118 (Mohr Siebeck, 2002). Richard Price offers an accessible review of the use of the "fathers" as proof of orthodoxy in Greek-speaking debates from the late fourth through seventh centuries.

As much as the collective weight of the fathers mattered in late antiquity, some fathers were weightier than others. Athanasius of Alexandria earned his reputation for being a defender of orthodoxy, mostly through his constant polemical writing, his demonization of those he considered enemies (first among them Arius), and his skillful political spin to reframe the five times he was removed or chased away from his bishopric and forced into exile.[12] As his authority grew, Athanasius's reputation for orthodoxy passed from a literary quality to an essential one. Seventy years after his death, here is how another bishop of Alexandria wrote about him:

> He brought joy throughout the world by his own writings, for he was attested by all as beyond mere correctness and accuracy of dogma.... In truth, the man is eminently worthy of our confidence, as he did not say anything that was not in agreement with Holy Scriptures. How indeed could he have erred from the truth?[13]

As he reflected back on the erstwhile bishop of his city, Cyril of Alexandria found Athanasius so correct, so orthodox, that not only did he not stray from what was right, it was not even thinkable that he might have strayed from what was right. Athanasius,

---

See Price, "Conciliar Theology: Resources and Limitations" in *Die Synoden im trinitarischen Streit: Über die Etablierung eines synodalen Verfahrens und die Probleme seiner Anwendung im 4. und 5. Jahrhundert*, ed. Uta Heil and Annette von Stockhausen, Texte und Untersuchungen 177 (De Gruyter, 2017).

12. On exile, see Jennifer Barry, *Bishops in Flight: Exile and Displacement in Late Antiquity* (University of California Press, 2019), esp. 31–55; on Athanasius's campaign against Arius, see Ellen Muehlberger, "The Legend of Arius's Death: Imagination, Space and Filth in Late Ancient Historiography," *Past & Present* 227 (2015): 3–29.

13. See Patrick T. R. Gray, "'The Select Fathers': Canonizing the Patristic Past." *Studia Patristica* 23 (1989): 21–36. This essay cites Cyril of Alexandria, *Ad Monachos Aegypti* (ACO I.1.1., 11ff; it is CPG 5301).

like a few others, had reached a new level of esteem among ancient Christian writers, even when considered among the collective of the fathers. These were the select fathers, men who had developed, as Patrick Gray observed, a kind of "superstar" status that outstripped even their illustrious peers, placing them far above other writers from the past.[14]

With that status came abundance. Corresponding to the increase in Christianity toward reverence for the fathers of the church was a commitment to anthologize their words (indeed, it is not clear whether the reverence or the anthologizing came first!). The writings of fathers, and especially select fathers, were the focus of collection, edition, and collation in antiquity. Florilegia abound in late antiquity, letter collections are shaped, sermon series are gathered and preserved, and in turn, the presence of these textual bodies for a particular father generated more authority for him as a father. In the case of Athanasius, a library of writings accumulated under his name, including the *Life of Antony*, his treatises on the Nicene controversy, and his festal letters.

Alongside the impulse to preserve any one man's words came the desire for more words. Athanasian texts are accompanied by something that, for understanding the appeal to the fathers, is equally important: a hefty selection of texts *attributed* to Athanasius, circulating in antiquity and transmitted to modernity under his name. There are over one hundred pieces listed in the *Clavis Patrum Graecorum* that were, at some point, incorrectly

14. Gray, "Select Fathers." Elsewhere, Gray details the case for the fathers' infallibility put forward by Leontius. See Gray, "Neo-Chalcedonianism and the Tradition: From Patristic to Byzantine Theology" (*Byzantinische Forschungen* 8 (1982): 61–70. To understand how the concept of celebrity might capture aspects of late ancient culture, see also Caroline T. Schroeder, "Exemplary Women," in *Melania: Early Christianity through the Life of One Family*, ed. C. M. Chin and Caroline T. Schroeder (University of California Press, 2017), 50–66.

attributed to Athanasius.[15] We can gauge his growing authority among the fathers by the size of this expansive catalog. The same goes for other early Christian writers like John Chrysostom or Basil of Caesarea or Augustine: the *dubia* and *spuria* attributed to them are also a sediment precipitated by their authority, so strong it draws new texts by these men into existence.

Thus, a father is, in this system, a force abundant, but uncontained, and that is where trouble can begin. The powerful guarantee that any select father's name conveyed was too much for the system of citation to bear. The more that the name came to mean, the less the content of what was said underneath that name actually mattered. Eventually, the disconnect between content and authority caused an accident that was already remarkable in its own time, but whose effects rippled out far into the future—the strange moment when a writer, himself taken as a lodestar of orthodoxy, championed a heretical position he misidentified as orthodox, because he imagined that a father like Athanasius had coined it.

II: THE ACCIDENT

Cyril of Alexandria lived from roughly 375 to 444 CE. Politically savvy and ready with tactics that sometimes shocked his contemporaries, Cyril was known above all as a fierce defender of orthodoxy. He was a primary actor in the controversy over the nomenclature for Mary, the mother of Jesus, which led to the Council of Ephesus in 431 CE, where his position was affirmed and that of his enemy Nestorius was condemned. After his death,

---

15. Athanasius's legitimate works are CPG 2090–2165; those listed as doubtful span 2171–2220; and those labeled spurious are 2230–2309.

Cyril became a hero to Christians who were otherwise divided by the decision of that council and the subsequent one in Chalcedon. Almost immediately considered one of the fathers of the church, Cyril inspired others, and his writings served many as a source of authority in argument and certainty in choppy theological waters. As Patrick Gray has detailed, bitter enemies, opponents with long-held grudges, all claimed the same Alexandrian bishop of the past as the progenitor of their positions.[16]

None of the later Christians who lay claim to Cyril and the legacy of his ideas were obviously out of bounds to do so, because Cyril had written a lot in his lifetime. He expressed himself in various ways amenable to a range of later interpretations. Like writers do, Cyril chose different approaches to different matters, investing more or less weight in an argument or using starker or softer registers to say what he meant. As thinkers do, Cyril developed and shifted his ideas in response to conversations, challenges, and persuasion by others. For example, the bellicose emotion on display in Cyril's *Third Letter to Nestorius*, written at a heated moment in a controversy known for its acrimony, would suggest that Cyril could never consider a more nuanced position, nor accept anything that might edge him toward what Nestorius and those with him were thinking. And yet, just a few short years later, he was willing to accept a statement that aimed to reconcile the two sides, easing back from a division that he was instrumental in creating in the first place![17]

---

16. Patrick T. R. Gray, *Claiming the Mantle of Cyril: Cyril of Alexandria and the Road to Chalcedon* (Peeters, 2021).

17. *Third Letter to Nestorius* and *Letter of Reunion*, both in *Christ: Through the Nestorian Controversy*, ed. Mark DelCogliano (Cambridge University Press, 2022), 623–36 and 718–25.

Move forward a few more years, and we find Cyril making a choice that would have far-reaching consequences. Having once more been called on to clarify his position about the nature of Christ—the entity Christians claimed to be at once the human, fleshly being Jesus and the eternal, incorporeal Word of God—Cyril adopted a peculiar phrase. In response to a challenge regarding the son's nature, Cyril affirmed that all Christians should agree that there is "one incarnate nature of the Word," which cannot be divided into two persons.[18] He presented the phrase as something secure, because it was "as the fathers have said"—meaning, this snippet of description came to Cyril with the guarantee of having been generated by an earlier, orthodox writer. Although he introduced it under the tag of the corporate plural, "fathers," Cyril took up the phrase knowing it as the words of Athanasius of Alexandria. A predecessor and the father Cyril revered as incapable of error, Athanasius had used it in a letter that he had written to explain his theological commitments to the emperor Jovian. Because it appeared in this most formal of settings—an apologetic letter of a bishop to an emperor—and because it came from the pen of a man whose correctness was by definition without flaw, the phrase offered the greatest assurance for a safe encapsulation of the Son's nature.

Except it was not. The letter that included this phrase circulated under the name of Athanasius, but it had been composed by

---

18. Cyril, *First Letter to Succensus* 6, in, *Cyril of Alexandria: Select Letters*, ed. Lionel R. Wickham, Oxford Early Christian Texts (Clarendon, 1983), 76: "μίαν φύσιν τοῦ λόγου σεσαρκωμένην." Others among Cyril's letters repeat the phrase or variations on it; see *To Eulogius* and *Second Letter to Succensus* 3, for example. The position captured by the phrase is complex, as is the debate surrounding it; narrating them here does not seem to help my point, but for a quick overview, see the introductions to Mark DelCogliano, ed., *Cambridge Editions of Early Christian Writings*, vols. 3 and 4 (Cambridge University Press, 2022).

someone else. It was one of many, many texts that had accumulated under the Alexandrian bishop's name. Already in antiquity, its author was identified as Apollinarius of Laodicea, or perhaps one of his followers. Apollinarius had been, at one time, Athanasius's ally; he was excommunicated by the emperor Constantius II for meeting with Athanasius in 346, when Athanasius was out of favor. By the 370s, however, Apollinarius's teachings had diverged from the positions held by Athanasius, and he had begun to create new, rival hierarchies of ordained men.[19] Quickly, the interpretation in antiquity became that Apollinarius or Apollinarians were attempting a deliberate fraud by writing texts under Athanasius's authority; knowing that their ideas could not pass muster without some aid, they labeled their texts with the name of the man considered the champion of orthodoxy.[20] Of course, a few texts slipped through, and thus, in a later defense of orthodox views, Cyril—the man who would be the fifth-century lodestar of orthodoxy for so many—took up and affirmed a phrase, five little words, that had come from the pen of a heretic from the fourth century. What is worse, Cyril himself did not even seem to recognize the controversial nature of what he was saying before he undertook to defend the phrase as orthodox, and he assigned it the authority of a writing from the fathers.

19. For an overview, the classic treatment is Hans Lietzmann, *Apollinaris von Laodicea und seine Schule: Texte und Untersuchungen* (Mohr Siebeck, 1904); a more recent edited volume offers a glimpse of where scholarship is now. See Silke-Petra Bergjan et al., *Apollinarius und seine Folgen*, Studien und Texte zu Antike und Christentum 93 (Mohr Siebeck, 2015).
20. See Theresia Hainthaler, "Die apollinaristischen Fälschungen und die christologischen Debatten des 5. und 6. Jahrhunderts: Einige Beobachtungen," in Bergjan et al., *Apollinarius und seine Folgen*, 269–84; A. Tuilier, "Remarques sur les frauds des Apollinaristes et des Monophysites: Notes de critique textuelle," in *Texte und Textkritik: Eine Aufsatzsammlung*, ed. Jürgen Dummer (Akademie Verlag, 1987), 581–90.

In that moment, the authority attributed to a father of the church clashed with the assumed orthodoxy of what a father of the church would say. Two irresistible forces met. If the existence of the fathers can be traced back to Athanasius's campaign to bolster his own authority by championing his interpretation of Nicaea, then the existence of the superfather can be traced to the accident that mangled the relationship between a father's authority and the orthodoxy of his words. The moment that Cyril, a father if there ever was one, adopted the phrase from the pseudo-Athanasian text and affirmed it with his own voice, he set in motion the creation of a new identity, one that would ultimately subsume him and begin to bend time around him.[21] In late ancient Christianity, there are Christians, there are writers, there are bishops and fathers and even select fathers. And then there are some who are still more than all that. There are *super*fathers.

The label of "superfather" may sound excessive, fantastic, maybe supernatural, like a superhero or a supersoldier. But a superfather is *super*—he exceeds every other kind of figure, in that he is not subject to the kinds of limits most human beings labor under, even the most lauded among us, like the "select fathers."[22]

---

21. If, while reading this, you think of Dr. Manhattan, you are correct: Alan Moore's *Watchmen* influenced how I read the acts of this council and Cyril's character at them, especially the issue "The Watchmaker," "Chapter 4," DC Comics, December 1986. For how superheroes' origin stories bend time, see Federico Pagello, "The 'Origin Story' is the Only Story: Seriality and Temporality in Superhero Fiction from Comics to Post-Television," *Quarterly Review of Film and Video* 34 (2017): 725–45. Sara Ronis demonstrates how useful superheroes are for thinking about human beings of extraordinary status in "It's a Roman . . . It's a Persian . . . It's Rabbi Meir: Secret Identities and the Rabbinic Self in the Babylonian Talmud," *Journal of Jewish Identities* 14 (2021): 93–110.

22. Gray's use of that label inspired me to think about differences in esteem among the writers claimed as "fathers" and at the same time left me wanting more as I tried to understand what happened at the Second Council of Constantinople. It is absolutely correct, but still insufficient to call someone

The superfather's existence changes the inclinations of individuals and groups, creating a new landscape for treating common ideas and interpretations of the past.

III: STRANGE NEW WORLD

In late antiquity, there were many responses to this striking moment in Cyril of Alexandria's career. Some saw in his expression the proof of their approach to understanding the nature of Christ, and thus their own opportunity to proceed with the support of a citation from a father of the church for their views. Others saw in it a mistake, in no small part brought about by Cyril's rash personality. From this perspective, Cyril swung too far as he attempted to avoid the problems with the Nestorian position, sweeping past the midline into an opposite, but still heretical, pole. Regardless of whether they saw in Cyril's adoption of the phrase an opportunity or a disaster, almost everyone recognized it as an anomaly, and it became a frequent topic of commentary or critique.

The sharpest, most extensive criticism survives in a document written by Ibas, a priest from Edessa. It is a letter addressed to a single individual; but, like many letters in the ancient world, it was meant to be read by many. That is to say, it was a kind of formal case against Cyril.[23] In it, Ibas tells a story of the 420s and 430s, describing the conflict Cyril was in with Nestorius when he first adopted the problematic phrase. Ibas maligns Cyril's judgment, but also his morals, accusing him of "evils" and "limitless effrontery" in his acts leading up to and during the Council of Ephesus.[24]

---

like Cyril a "superstar," as it is clear that we are dealing with something more than wider fame or more intense celebrity or even greater authority.

23. Price, *Acts of Constantinople*, 1:88.
24. Ibas, *Letter to Mari* 6–7 (*Acts of Constantinople*, 2:9).

This letter was reviewed at the following council, at Chalcedon, where its author was also in attendance. Ultimately, fault was not found with the message or the messenger.

One hundred years later, however, this relatively short document was reevaluated, precisely because it described Cyril as having erred in his expressions about the nature of Christ. In what Price has labeled as the "most intricate and most bizarre part" of the Second Council of Constantinople's review of past writings, Ibas's letter was reasoned to be a forgery because of two things that were seen as mutually exclusive. First, the letter criticized Cyril for going too far and following the path laid by Apollinarius when he tried to argue against Nestorius, but then, its author Ibas had been chastised, reviewed, and ultimately affirmed as orthodox by the Council of Chalcedon. If the letter critiquing Cyril were authentic, then the bishops who gathered at Chalcedon had affirmed something that had suggested Cyril had dipped into heresy. Indeed, the letter was left to stand. But after Chalcedon, Cyril's status had grown so immense that the presence of this critique from a writer the assembly at Chalcedon had reviewed and accepted was untenable. And unacceptable—so much so that the Second Council of Constantinople, itself also invested in the authority of conciliar decisions, declared a previously unquestioned and ostensibly authentic document to be a forgery, in order to resolve the impasse of Cyril's use of a different, unrecognized forgery as if it were authentic and orthodox. Rather than allowing that Cyril may have made a mistake, the Second Council of Constantinople considered the matter and interpreted the phrase as orthodox, Cyril as unflawed, and Ibas's letter to be a forgery.[25]

25. Here the emperor Justinian set the agenda, with his multiple writings about the correct approach issued before the council. *On the Orthodox Faith* survives intact, and it devotes a significant amount of space, not to mention

In the scholarship about the emerging habit of citing and trusting the fathers of the church, there is widespread puzzlement about this kind of strategy. How can a culture that has turned to authenticity and tradition also employ the notion of forgery so quickly and seemingly without attachment to accuracy? Across multiple studies, a single pronouncement resounds. Writing on the late ancient development of pseudepigraphical texts, Matthieu Cassin notes that it is "paradoxal" that the rise of the "father" as a guarantor of orthodoxy is accompanied by so many texts that ride falsely under the names of those fathers.[26] Yonatan Moss, working on developments in the early 500s, saw a different way that these new citational customs bore "a tinge of paradox."[27] As he puts it, "the more revered a text, the more liable it is to be corrupted"—that is, to be adapted to new ideas rather than preserved as is from the time of expression as an authentic product of the father whose authority it draws on. Robin Whelan has written extensively of the imagined dialogues created by late ancient Christians, starring otherwise long-dead men who speak to address the heresies that have developed since their deaths. These dialogues have a "paradoxical relationship" with the culture of citations from the fathers, as they "simultaneously traded on the clout of church Fathers and flouted the rules of patristic citation by attributing to

---

one very well-placed ellipsis, to showing that the phrase "one incarnate nature of the Word" does *not*, in fact, demonstrate that Cyril assented to the idea that Christ had one nature.

26. Matthieu Cassin, "Citer, collecter: florilèges et citations d'auteurs patristiques dans les controverses doctrinales," part 2, *Annuaire de l'EPHE, section des Sciences religieuses* (2022): 277: "Il est cependant paradoxal que cet appel à l'autorité de foi des saints pères s'appuie en réalité si souvent sur des documents pseudépigraphes, qui reviennent en fait à des auteurs condamnés par l'Église dont se réclame Cyrille, à savoir Apolinaire et plusieurs de ses disciples."

27. Moss, "'Packed with Patristic Testimonies,'" 240.

them new words and ideas," material they had never, and could never have, written.[28] The chorus of "paradox!" coming from so many different scholars about different contexts signals that there appear to be two guiding principles at work here, side by side, where accuracy and authenticity underwrite the value of textual citation but are *not* the criteria that govern judgments about whether something is a forgery or not.

It is no surprise that the actions at the Second Council of Constantinople have drawn this kind of commentary, too. The historian Susan Wessel, for example, revisits the charges of forgery, and the actual practice of forgery, that hover around Cyril of Alexandria, in her essay, "Literary Forgery and the Monothelete Controversy: Some Scrupulous Uses of Deception."[29] She notes that the council's participants must have understood its forgeries "in characteristically paradoxical terms." Forgery, she observes, was "both a rhetorical charge that could be leveled against adversaries to remove certain texts from theological discussion, and simultaneously a means by which one could alter texts to make them consistent with one's most deeply held beliefs."[30] But the actions have their own logic and she cautions that late ancient Christians using and declaring forgery did so scrupulously—they "did not 'intend to deceive'" their audiences in the way that most modern scholars assume.[31]

---

28. Robin Whelan, "Surrogate Fathers: Imaginary Dialogue and Patristic Culture in Late Antiquity," *Early Medieval Europe* 25 (2017): 36.

29. Susan Wessel, *Greek, Roman, and Byzantine Studies* 42 (2001): 201, also citing Bruce Metzger, "Literary Forgeries and Canonical Pseudepigrapha," *Journal of Biblical Literature* 91 (1972): 3–24. Much of this scholarship qualifies what is happening as "literary," which is another way of softening the description of what is happening.

30. Susan Wessel, "Literary Forgery and the Monothelete Controversy: Some Scrupulous Uses of Deception," *Greek, Roman and Byzantine Studies* 42 (2001): 201–20, at 219–20.

31. Wessel, "Scrupulous Uses," 219.

Patrick Gray's essay "Covering the Nakedness of Noah: Reconstruction and Denial in the Age of Justinian" has a similar aim, though he squares the circle differently.[32] Working over the same materials (the multiple forgeries, charges of forgery, and obviously false accusations of forgery around Cyril of Alexandria and in the Second Council of Constantinople), Gray sees, like Wessel, that forgery as a practice was a way for late ancient Christians to manage a tension—namely, that between the desire for continuity and the inexorable necessity of change.[33] Gray speaks of Christians as complex, each engaging in what he calls the "double movement" of "reconstruction and denial."[34] There are not two kinds of people (say, on the one hand, those who fake and forge, while on the other, those who are innocent and often victims of others' fakery); rather, it is the same people who are at once insisting on the authenticity of forged documents supporting their position and picking apart, in quite expert fashion, the forgeries attempted by their opponents.

Gray's evidence for teasing out late ancient Christian motivations arrives in the form of a repeated allusion. His sources return, multiple times, to the story of the drunken Noah from Genesis 9. In the biblical passage, Noah drinks, then passes out naked, and two of his sons manage to cover him without seeing his naked body by walking backward over where he sleeps, dragging a blanket over him as they go. Given how often the story appears in late ancient Christian writing around forgery, Gray argues, "it should come as no surprise if the image of the covering of Noah's nakedness really does, as we have speculated, reveal the

32. Patrick T. R. Gray, "Covering the Nakedness of Noah: Reconstruction and Denial in the Age of Justinian," *Byzantinische Forschung* 24 (1997): 193–206.
33. Gray, "Covering the Nakedness of Noah," 193.
34. Gray, "Covering the Nakedness of Noah," 196.

age's repressed, subconscious, or semi-conscious tension about its reconstruction of the religious past in its struggle to achieve conformity."[35] From there, psychological language pervades Gray's analysis of the situation: there are "projections" and awareness at a "half-conscious" level of what is being done; there are "repressions" and "denials" and "double-think." This is the measure of his consistent surprise, as well as detached irony, at the demonstrably untrue assertions by his subjects. Gray lays all his weight on the mode of psychology, as the "double movement" or double awareness or misrecognition is the diagnosis; however, it gives no deeper historical or contextual analysis apart from that to explain why people might have slipped into this kind of state.[36]

Both Gray and Wessel are attempting to make space for readers to accept the compositional practices of antiquity that clearly diverge from our expectations. Their goal is both laudable and understandable, given that modern discussions of forgery impart the assumption of both deviance and deception to the craft. In his 1990 book, *Forgers and Critics*, Anthony Grafton set the tone, moralizing about forgery in stark terms. Grafton identified a difference between two classes of writers: critics engage in analysis of texts, interpretation of their circumstances; forgers do that, too, but to different ends. "Forgery is a sort of crime," Grafton tells us, so we should understand what these "great

---

35. Gray, "Covering the Nakedness of Noah," 196.

36. For more evidence of the impulse to wonder about the motivations of forgers, see Einar Thomassen, review of *Forgery and Counterforgery*, by Bart D. Ehrman, *Journal of Theological Studies* n.s. 65 (2014): 243, cited by Brakke, "Lying Liars," 383. Richard Price does his own version of psychologizing in "Malleable Past," as cited by Thomas Graumann, "Orthodoxy, Authority, and Reconstruction of the Past in Church Councils," in *Invention, Rewriting, Usurpation: Discursive Fights over Religious Traditions in Antiquity*, ed. Jörg Ulrich et al., Early Christianity in the Context of Antiquity 11 (Peter Lang, 2011).

sinners" are doing by considering their "crimes" as an investigator would: by looking for motive, means, and opportunity.[37] This makes critics (and the readers who would identify with them) into the police, and so critical examinations should be guided by the norms of policing. Grafton explains that just as police might think "it takes a thief to catch a thief," so too it "takes a forger to expose a fake."[38] The moralizing redounds to that detective, the critic: as the detective *and* the upright citizen, he performs what Grafton calls a "vital" profession, whose practice "is a sign of health and vitality in a civilization; the prevalence of forgery is a sign of illness and vice."[39] When the book was reissued just a few years ago, Grafton doubled down on the policing language, writing in the 2018 afterword that "the robbers were ahead of the cops in antiquity and they still are."[40]

Undergirding this moral framework is the idea that behind every text is a writer who intends to represent themselves and their sources truthfully or falsely. Indeed, intention has been the guiding concept in scholarly estimations of texts and their authenticity. German scholar Armin Daniel Baum offered a multilevel taxonomy of pseudepigraphy, where intent intervenes on each level and creates a new subclassification between intended and

---

37. Anthony Grafton, *Forgers and Critics: Creativity and Duplicity in Western Scholarship* (Princeton University Press, 1990), 37; cf. the reference to forgers' "crime(s)" on 78; their "dishonest living" on 41.

38. Grafton, *Forgers and Critics*, 123; cf. Irene Peirano, *Rhetoric of the Roman Fake: Latin Pseudepigrapha in Context* (Oxford University Press, 2012), 7–8.

39. Grafton, *Forgers and Critics*, 127; Javier Martínez, "Pseudepigraphy," in *A Companion to Late Antique Literature*, ed. Scott McGill and Edward J. Watts (Wiley, 2018), 402. Martínez ("Pseudepigraphy," 402) notes Grafton's insistence on the noninnocence of forgers (*Forgers and Critics*, 37).

40. Grafton, *Forgers and Critics*, afterword.

unintended falsity.⁴¹ To this, Javier Martínez suggests adding other qualifications. He presents them as advancements beyond Baum's focus on intent, but each one—"parody, plagiarism, interpolations and alterations, commissioned texts, and ghostwriting"—centers yet again the circumstances of composition and, with them, the motives of the composer.⁴² Setting aside direct statements about authors' intentions, the enticement of there being some person, some creator that we might know and through whom we might discern an intent, is also visible in the language scholars use about the practice of forgery: it is an "instrument," a "strategy," a "tool," words that point back to the wielder of the tool. At that point the hunt for the author and his intention resumes.⁴³

With this sorting mechanism in hand to identify a text, it is then a matter of discernment. Or *asking*, as Bart Ehrman wonders:

41. Martínez ("Pseudepigraphy," 402) describes it like this: "The typology of pseudepigraphy has been detailed in an exemplary manner by Baum (2001), who distinguishes between primary pseudepigrapha, those whose author deliberately appends a false name to the text, and secondary, where various factors might attach the wrong author's name to a work in the course of transmission. Baum offers two other useful criteria: whether the ascription is deliberate or not and whether it is intentionally or unintentionally deceptive."

42. Peirano criticizes this focus, noting that the term *forgery* can come with a range of negative connotations, but *pseudepigrapha* can be ambivalent: the "pseudo-" of the prefix can mean false, as in wrong, or false, as in deceitful. See Peirano, *Rhetoric of the Roman Fake*, 1.

43. See, for instance, Patrick T. R. Gray, "Forgery as an Instrument of Progress: Reconstructing the Theological Tradition in the Sixth Century," *Byzantinische Zeitschrift* 81 (1988): 284–89. In this piece, Gray notes that Christians did not see their own obviously forged texts as forged, and that it was not a matter of lacking the critical tools to do so, as they quickly identified the forgeries of others. As he puts it, "Some other dynamic was operative here to allow this simultaneous critique of opponents' forgeries and the maintenance of their own" (285). See also Andrew S. Jacobs, "'Solomon's Salacious Song': Foucault's Author Function and the Early Christian Interpretation of the Canticum Canticorum," *Medieval Encounters* 4 (1998): 1–23.

why would an author "choose to lie about his identity?"[44] That is, to classify works without authors in this system, we still need to investigate the author's motives, in part to recover or rehabilitate some of the works, those that do not necessarily *mean* to deceive, while leaving others in the bin, because they were composed with the intent to deceive. Some historians are unable to make the religious subject matter of many of these texts cohere with their obvious aim to misrepresent their origins or provenance or authorship. This is what leads to categories like "pious fraud" or Wolfgang Speyer's "real religious pseudepigraphy," by which he means a writer so caught up in the writing that he cannot help but pretend to be someone else writing the text.[45] When it is a matter of evaluating Christian texts, intention matters—or at least, intention has mattered to scholars. Essays about the heyday of forgery in late antiquity strive to square the circle, explaining how Christians and especially Christian theologians involved in forgery did not forge with bad intentions.

Of course, these concerns have always sat a little oddly alongside the literary history of Christianity, which is not just full of forgery but perhaps even defined by it. As Ehrman pithily observed, "the most distinctive feature of the early Christian literature is the extent to which it was forged."[46] There is a distinct disconnect between the creation of texts in the earliest centuries of the movement and their association with authors that are not their own: The Gospels of Matthew, Mark, Luke, and John are not by any "Matthew," "Mark," "Luke," or

---

44. Bart D. Ehrman, *Forgery and Counterforgery: The Use of Literary Deceit in Early Christian Polemics* (Oxford University Press, 2012), 4.

45. For a discussion of the extensions of this, see Brakke, "Lying Liars," 378–90.

46. Ehrman, *Forgery and Counterforgery*, 1.

"John"; "Paul's" letter to the Hebrews was attributed to but not penned by Paul; Revelation was not written by John of Patmos as tradition would have it; the Epistle of Barnabas, the Gospel of Judas, the Acts of Paul and Thecla—none of them originate with their titled characters. Even in later antiquity, David Brakke writes, "Christians seem to have embraced the practice with special enthusiasm."[47] As Christians gained power, the "proliferat[ion]" and "dissemination" of forged texts "picked up speed from the fourth century onward, seemingly prompted by the religious controversies that arose after Christianity had become the official religion of the empire."[48]

Forgeries allowed Christian writers to accomplish many things they desired, but they were especially useful in the project of perpetual adjustment in late ancient Christian culture—its penchant for inventing the textual, ritual, and material evidence necessary to authenticate the emerging narrative Christians were creating about their past.[49] Edicts were drawn up and attributed to emperors who did not issue them, making them say what should have been said;[50] stories were made up and then set in the past in order to justify emerging anti-Jewish politics as something original to Christianity and necessary for Christian piety;[51] diaries

---

47. Brakke, "Lying Liars," 378.

48. J. Martínez, "Pseudepigraphy," 404, picking up on what Brakke identifies as the "conflict model" ("Lying Liars," 381) in Ehrman's thought.

49. Ellen Muehlberger, "Perpetual Adjustment: The *Passion of Perpetua and Felicity* and the Entailments of Authenticity," *Journal of Early Christian Studies* 30 (2022): 313–42.

50. See Clifford Ando, "Pagan Apologetics and Christian Intolerance in the Ages of Themistius and Augustine," *Journal of Early Christian Studies* 4 (1996): 178.

51. Paul C. Dilley, "The Invention of Christian Tradition: 'Apocrypha,' Imperial Policy, and Anti-Jewish Propaganda," *Greek, Roman, & Byzantine Studies* 50 (2010): 586–615.

were invented to provide audiences with the experiences of martyrs long commemorated in ritual;[52] visions were recounted to place emerging late ancient Christian ideas about the dead in the mouths of venerable first-century figures;[53] documents were composed to portray church organization as timeless, stable from the very earliest moments when followers of Jesus gathered;[54] and existing texts were expanded and shaped to match the needs of the moment.[55]

IV: WE CAN REBUILD HIM, WE HAVE THE TECHNOLOGY

The Christian project of inventing the past includes inventing a past full of perfectly orthodox writers: the fathers, called upon as a repository of correct thought at the moment they are being created. While studies of the appeal to the fathers have often termed it a "literary" phenomenon, there comes a time when the merely literary passes into the ontological.[56] Some of the fathers become

---

52. Muehlberger, "Perpetual Adjustment."

53. Ellen Muehlberger, *Moment of Reckoning: Imagined Death and Its Consequences in Late Ancient Christianity* (Oxford University Press, 2019), esp. chapter 4, "What Remains? Situating the Postmortal."

54. See Pauliina Pylvänäinen, *Agents in Liturgy, Charity and Communication: The Tasks of Female Deacons in the Apostolic Constitutions*, Studia Traditionis Theologiae 37 (Brepols, 2020).

55. Paul R. Gilliam, *Ignatius of Antioch and the Arian Controversy* (Brill, 2017), esp. chapter 1, "The Arian Controversy and the 'Authentic' Letters of Ignatius of Antioch," 8–48.

56. Cf. Wessel, "Scrupulous Uses"; Bruce Metzger, "Literary Forgeries and Canonical Pseudepigrapha," *Journal of Biblical Literature* 91 (1972): 3–24. Cf. also Ehrman's subtitle, *The Use of Literary Deceit in Early Christian Polemics*, or Vessey, "Forging of Orthodoxy," 496n2, where he calls this "dogmatical fixation" "a specific phenomenon of Christian *literature*" (my emphasis) and, interestingly, not a matter of the factual or theological order. He attempts to

hyperpious, constitutionally incapable of error. When a writer is esteemed, his words weigh more than others and can be used to shore up a position against its varied, available opponents. When a writer is so esteemed that he can no longer say something wrong, he has no discernible choices, thus no intention, strategy, or agency; he is no longer a writer, at least if we are looking for a person with a pen and a plan.[57] When the entire machinery of a council works to align a father's varied statements with a single position, he surpasses even the category of "father."

What are the characteristics of this being? First, a superfather inhabits a different kind of body than other important authorities, like bishops or fathers. Every superfather is related to someone who inhabited a body of flesh; that person, whatever he may have written during his lifetime, no longer exists when a superfather in his name comes into being. In his new state, though, he is not bound by the limits of corporeal existence. In fact, he is usually created after the death of the body, by the labor of readers who interpret him, cultivate and edit his works, and insist on his status. Once created, the superfather survives *only* by the work of others, over years and centuries. The prevalence of collected dossiers of work may be seen as a reanimation, the corpus of approved writings standing (almost literally) in the place of the now-lost body of the man. And that new body can grow and expand as new texts are attributed to him—superfathers tend to acquire new writings as time goes on—and wilder still, new

---

explain, saying, "exactly how and why this change occurred are important and difficult questions of Christian *literary* history" (502).

57. This is the point at which Foucault's author function will spring to mind, but Vessey's analysis of the mistaken foundations of that essay show Jerome enjoying a status approaching that of superfather (see "Forging of Orthodoxy," esp. 506–8).

conversations of his are recorded.[58] A superfather does not need a mouth to speak or a hand to write, as he has, and lives through, the hands and mouths of others.

Nor is the superfather subject to the constraints of time. I mean this basically, in terms of lifespan, as he lives beyond the normal terms of a human life. But I also mean it more complexly, in terms of the direction of time's flow and, with it, causality. Once created, a superfather changes how other Christians act going forward, but his presence also changes the past that has already happened. It is good to remember that a superfather blots out the human being that preceded him and was his seed. For example, a historian could look at Cyril of Alexandria the man and watch him make irregular, sometimes irrational decisions during his life, see as he takes on multiple, often conflicting interpretations, and take note, even as he unknowingly, then perhaps knowingly, adopts falsely attributed and heretical ideas. That Cyril is eminently human; he cannot even recognize a rather blatant misattribution.[59] The difference between the living man whose thinking evolved and the unlimited authority granted the superfather who is, by definition, already correct can seem like an occasion for hypocrisy, on

58. Whelan, "Surrogate Fathers" is the most important rendering of this, but there are many, many examples of dead men brought back to speak anew. See also Paola Buzi, "Codices Coptici Rescripti: A Preliminary Census of the Palimpsests from the White Monastery," in The Rediscovery of Shenoute: Studies in Honor of Stephen Emmel, ed. Anne Boud'hours et al. (Peeters, 2022), 180, where she describes a late dialogue between Basil of Caesarea and Gregory of Nazianzus.

59. The phrase Cyril lifted may seem obscure, as if it sent no signal, but its oddness with respect to what Cyril was previously known for supporting was likely clear to most people in the know in his time. Translated to our own context, it might be like finding a person who had become convinced that it was an Ann Arbor tradition to insist on labeling our school "THE University of Michigan," when that is in fact a laughable tic of Our Neighbors to the South and something recognizable to most people who have a stake in our rivalry.

the part of Cyril's supporters, or even duplicity. But it is better to recognize the shift in, for lack of a better phrase, the ontological status of the superfather "Cyril," and to watch as that new being expands both backward and forward to affect all of time.

Alongside the odd deployment of forgery charges at the council there was a second indicator that the world had shifted around the emerging superfather. Some Christians began to use a new and controversial approach, reading back into the past to judge men who were long dead for their orthodoxy in current debates. Posthumous condemnation had been roundly rejected, even as late as the mid-fifth century. For instance, the powerful bishop Cyril of Alexandria explained in his lifetime that a retroactive evaluation of men now dead to see whether they lived up to newer ideals was just not worth it. "I yield," he wrote, "to those who think it a serious matter to revile the dead, even if they are laymen, and all the more if they departed from this life in the episcopacy."[60] Cyril would rather leave the dead to the dead. The emperor at the time, Theodosius II, was also concerned about the practice, imagining the disruption that an interrogation of the past could bring. He therefore urged a group of Syrian bishops to let things lie for the sake of good community. "What could be more useful," Theodosius wrote, "than that you resolve together with the whole church that no one should presume in future to do anything of the kind against those who died in her peace?"[61] So, near the middle of the fifth century, it was distasteful to look back and explicitly evaluate the orthodoxy of the dead who had been approved while alive.[62]

---

60. Cyril of Alexandria, *Letter* 91 (*Acts of Constantinople*, 1:69). See also his *Letter* 106.17 or 108.34.

61. Thedosius II, *In Facundas* VIII 3.13 (*Acts of Constantinople*, 1:275).

62. The Letter to Facundas is dated to 438 CE. *Implicitly*, however, we could look at the lionizing done in *vitae* as another channel by which the dead are

Even in the years just before the Second Council of Constantinople, there was still a consensus that posthumous condemnation simply was not done. The emperor Justinian raised the prospect and the response was pitched. One Pontianus, a bishop from North Africa, wrote directly to the emperor to say that his call to condemn the thought, and even the very person, of men long since passed away "disturbs us not a little." It seemed strange to Pontianus in the winter of 544–45 to "subject to a precipitate condemnation the authors of these words, who are already dead." His concern reveals the mechanisms expected in such a condemnation. He asks how it would all work. "If they were still living and, when corrected, would not condemn their own error, they would most justly be condemned. But as things are, to whom will our verdict of condemnation be read? There is nothing in them that could now be set right."[63] For him, there was no purpose a correction of the dead could have, because he interpreted the correction as something that was supposed to have consequence for *them*, the men condemned, and their punishing loss would only be possible while they were alive. To take up a posthumous condemnation was aggressive, even bellicose. As Pontianus explains, "And why should we declare war on the dead, where there is no victory to be won by combat? They are now in the hands of the true judge, from whom there is no appeal."[64] The dead are dead and they are gone.

---

aligned with the present. On this, see the illuminating essay on Gerontius's *Life of Melania*: Christine Shepardson, "Posthumous Orthodoxy," in Chin and Schroeder, *Melania: Early Christianity through the Life of One Family*.

63. Pontianus, *Letter to Justinian* (*Acts of Constantinople*, 1:111; PL 67:995–98, with these passages all on 997).

64. Price, *Acts of Constantinople*, 1:112; PL 67:998. These comments point to the fact that Pontianus does not envision the condemnation of men to have an effect on anyone but those men themselves; there is not yet for him a

Or they should be. Part of the reaction to Justinian's initiative to reach back and condemn people who had already died was fueled by the prospect of those people becoming *undead*, so to speak. The church and its traditions were, using a scriptural allusion, "a fountain sealed," as one Roman deacon put it.[65] As he wrote to his colleagues about the problem of posthumous condemnation, that deacon imagined its absurd implications, thinking of pious predecessors exiting their tombs to speak, upbraiding people who had not yet been born during their lifetimes for condemning them long after they had lived.[66] The line of argument from dissenters to Justinian's move is that condemnation is for the living, because the living can be chastised and corrected. Justinian was stretching time and, according to his critics, bringing the discourse into the strangest kind of presentism, where chronological boundaries collapse and ultimately tradition cannot stand. A kind of temporal vertigo was affecting everyone, such that dead men were imagined to speak in order to defend against dead men being judged. That new chronological expanse overpowered prior practice, even prior councils. Cyril's own words were declared a forgery when they conflicted with the strange new world where Cyril could not be wrong.[67]

These are the influences of the new type of being that emerged fully into the light at the council. A force of such strength does not

---

metaphysical structure in which such a condemnation would matter, though there seems to be one operative in Justinian's imagination.

65. Fulgentius Ferrandus, *Letter* 6.2 (Price 1:113; PL 67:922: *Fons est signatus*).

66. Fulgentius Ferrandus, *Letter* 6.4 (Price 1:115; PL 67:923: *"Quid si procedentes e tumulis suis coram Deo qui vivunt apud quem fideliter requiescunt in novissima resurrectione dicant viri religiosi."* In Ferrandus's letter, the pious ancestors give a long speech, roughly 250 words, as he ventriloquizes his arguments in their mouths.

67. Price, *Acts of Constantinople*, 1:276.

dissipate. In Cyril's case, the prevalence of forgery around him that has so puzzled scholars can be tied to his formation—what other way to transform a human writer into a superfather but to assiduously add to and subtract from the record that constitutes his thought and approves him? Instead of the Second Council of Constantinople being an embarrassment for patristic authority, it is the place where the community agrees (or almost all of them do) to embody and maintain a new superfather. It is Cyril's summoning into existence, his event of generation. Thus, forgery—in its use or its accusation—is in Christian tradition merely a step in shaping a superfather. When considered as a part of a literary practice, forgery appears to be driven by a value for accuracy and authenticity, but when it is part of solidifying an emerging superfather, it is accomplishing something entirely else. Theology takes center stage at ecumenical councils, and this council may not be any different: even the condemnation of the writers of the past styled "the Three Chapters" is less a matter of condemning their theology than condemning their explicit or implicit challenge to Cyril.

Thinking about late ancient Christian culture with the superfather is a way to get the history right, or at the very least a way to get the history to make sense. With it in hand, we are not left with a feeling of confusion—or worse, derision—about how the actors of the past behaved. We do not have to discount any part of the past as unserious or fallen or declining. The Second Council of Constantinople in 553, around which this essay has orbited, can be seen as no less important than other councils, not Ephesus or Chalcedon, not Nicaea; it is no more or less formal, no more or less an expression of piety, than any other communal decision made by late ancient Christians.

CHAPTER FOUR

Faces in the Crowds

*The So-Called Fayyum Portraits
and the Aftereffects of Photography*

They each look out at us from a roughly cut wood panel: A bearded priest with full, thick hair wears a diadem with a seven-pointed star. A boy with small lips and the slightest of smiles is identified by the writing on his clothing: Eutyches, freed person of Kasianos. An unadorned woman with close-set serious eyes and shadows beneath them has her dark hair carefully pulled back and perhaps braided on top. Another woman, by contrast, is bedecked with every finery—large gold earrings and a necklace set off her rosy face and enormous eyes. And scattered across the museums and institutions of North America and Europe are hundreds more of these, the so-called Fayyum portraits, painted in the villages of Egypt between 100 and 500 CE to commemorate the dead.[1]

The title alludes to Stewart Guthrie's famous work, *Faces in the Clouds: A New Theory of Religion* (Oxford University Press, 1995), where he argues that religion arises when humans anthropomorphize the environment, seeing agency in "faces" that do not exist.

1. In order, these are the portraits classified in Susan Walker, ed. *Ancient Faces: Mummy Portraits from Roman Egypt* (Routledge, 1997), as #21 (59–60,

Though these objects were created in the ancient world, they have a consistent effect on modern viewers, who perceive in them an "unsettling presence" bearing an "uncanny vitality."[2] A faint, but faithful, signal of a human presence at long remove is seen in "the haunting aspect of the gaze" they display.[3] "It is," one critic writes, "as if they have just tentatively stepped toward us."[4] Still others confirm these sensations, remarking how the pieces "almost uncannily bring before us individuals" and are "so lifelike we expect to run into them in Harvard Square."[5] Though the portraits were created in a funerary context, the faces in them are imagined to be just on the verge of speech, and it is to us that they will speak when they do, these "images of men and women making no appeal, asking for nothing, yet declaring themselves ... alive!"[6]

BM EA74714), #65 (103–105, New York Metropolitan Museum 1918 18.9.2), #34 (75, Berlin Staatliche Museen, Antikensammlung 31161/9), and #49 (88–89, Paris Louvre MND 2047 [P217]). Klaus Parlasca created an extensive catalog of over a thousand of these portraits in *Mumienporträts und verwandte Denkmaler* (Steiner, 1966). See also Vincent Rondot, *Derniers visages des dieux d'Egypte: iconographies, pantheons et cults dans le Fayoum hellénisé des IIe-IIIe siècles de notre ère* (Louvre, 2013); Barbara E. Borg, *Mumienporträts: Chronologie und Kultureller Kontext* (Philip von Zabern, 1996), *"Der zierlichste Anblick der Welt": Ägyptischen Porträtmumien* (Philip von Zabern, 1998); and "Painted Funerary Portraits," in the *UCLA Encyclopedia of Egyptology*, ed. Willeke Wendrich et al. (University of California, Los Angeles, 2010).

2. For "unsettling presence," see Euphrosyne Doxiadis, "Technique," in Walker, *Ancient Faces*, 30; for "uncanny vitality," see John Berger, *Portraits: John Berger on Artists* (Verso, 2015), 8.

3. Lorelei H. Corcoran and Marie Svoboda, *Herakleides: A Portrait Mummy from Roman Egypt* (Getty Trust, 2010), 19.

4. Berger, "Fayum Portrait Painters," in Berger, *Portraits*, 9.

5. Philipe de Montebello, "Director's Foreward [sic]," in Walker, *Ancient Faces*, 7; Kathleen M. Coleman, "Portraits of Loss," in *Funerary Portraits from Roman Egypt: Facing Forward*, digital companion to 2022 Harvard exhibition of the same name.

6. Berger, "Fayum Portrait Painters," in Berger, *Portraits*, 11. Cf. the title of Jean-Christophe Bailly's book-length essay on the portraits: *L'apostrophe*

Another writer, visiting an exhibition, recounts how she sensed a life force in them:

> An experience I had in Berlin convinced me of the power inherent in the best of the Fayum faces: I was left in a storage room on my own with about twenty portraits, and when the door closed behind me, I felt a very strange sensation—that I was not alone. None of these portraits was still on its mummy, and yet they transmitted the energy of human beings.[7]

All these reactions come from twentieth-century viewers, but they echo what was said when the portraits were first put on display in London in 1888. As Dominic Montserrat reports, "the first visitors to the exhibition commented on the living, breathing quality of the images."[8] At the time, the critic for the *Saturday Review* claimed after the show that the portraits were "perfectly startling in their lifelike appearance"; another reviewer imagined "the glow of life" on their faces, calling them the "veritable portraiture" of the people they depicted.[9]

The pieces do accomplish what portraiture usually does: they depict individuals, typically from the neck or shoulders up, with a focus on the face, in enough detail that no two are likely to be the same. The variation among the hundreds of surviving Fayyum portraits and their realistic style make it easy for viewers to see in them both life expressed as a general force and *lives* parceled out in individuality. Given these characteristics, we should not be surprised that the portraits have on multiple occasions evoked

---

muette: *Essai sur les portraits du Fayoum* (Éditions Hazan, 1997).

7. Euphrosyne Doxiadis, *The Mysterious Fayum Portraits from Ancient Egypt* (Abrams, 1995), 12.

8. Montserrat, "'To make death beautiful': The Other Life of the Fayum Portraits," *Apollo* 150 (July 1999): 20.

9. *Saturday Review*, June 1888, 792; John Forbes-Robinson, *Illustrated London News*, June 30, 1888, both cited by Montserrat, "'To make death beautiful,'" 20.

comparison to a different, slightly more modern genre of representation: to some, the portraits look like nothing so much as "passport photos," their styling "as frontal as pictures from a photo-mat."[10] With that resonance comes a guarantee; the portraits show simple faces, each slightly different, facing front; each bears "a placidity, a neutrality" in their look, and thus can convince viewers that they have the "objective neutrality of identification photos."[11] It is an apt comparison—the portraits *do* look like modern identification photos.

Part of what motivates the comparison to photography is, of course, style: the composition of the image, the disposition on the face of the person represented. But the portraits also resemble photography in what they are assumed to represent. In his book on the genre of photography and its effects, *Camera Lucida*, Roland Barthes observed that "every photograph is a certificate of presence."[12] It can seem that photographs consistently prove the reality of their contents: a photograph's effect is "to attest that what I see has indeed existed."[13] In this way, too, the Fayyum portraits are imagined to work: they appear to stand as evidence for us of real people and their lives in antiquity. Jumping the boundaries of time and space, these portraits seem to be windows through

---

10. Berger, "Fayum Portrait Painters," in Berger, *Portraits*, 8, 9.

11. Bailly, *L'apostrophe muette*, 70, 139. By contrast, James Fenton compares the portraits to "mug shots and passport photos" to bring out what he finds distinct about them. See Fenton, "The Mummy's Secret," *New York Review of Books*, July 17, 1997, 12–13.

12. Roland Barthes, *Camera Lucida: Reflections on Photography*, trans. Richard Howard (Hill and Wang, 1981), 87.

13. Barthes, *Camera Lucida* 82, cf. 87. Ariella Aïsha Azoulay places photography in the longer context of Columbian contact and conquest in "Toward the Abolition of Photography's Imperial Rights," in *Capitalism and the Camera: Essays in Photography and Extraction*, ed. Kevin Coleman and Daniel James (Verso, 2021), 27–54. I am grateful to Greg Given for directing me to her essay.

which we modern people might be able to spy individuals from late ancient Egypt.

That is a remarkable promise, but it is an illusion. The portraits as we encounter them are in fact modern European objects, created to answer modern European (and North American) desires and sensibilities. Although they go under the shorthand of "portraits" and are at times claimed as evidence of ancient traditions of painting, they were produced within the parameters of photography, which primed nineteenth-century antiquities dealers to see value in faces and has influenced the reception of these objects ever since. A "Fayyum portrait," then, is a kind of affective machine, which generates predictable responses from the viewers it was created to enthrall.[14]

In what follows, I will prove my case by first detailing the production of the portraits in the late nineteenth century, then examining two different ways that the reception of the portraits cashed in on epistemological promises specific to photography—that it could provide genealogical and reproductive evidence of origins. Finally, I will reflect on how the Fayyum portrait phenomenon is a representation of the more general relationship between knowledge, evidence, and the fascination that accompanies the study of the ancient world.

I: MAKING FACES

At the turn of the recent millennium, these extraordinary objects were the focus of not one, but two international exhibitions. The

---

14. And, indeed, only a small number of them are from the Fayyum, with most of them coming from other parts of village Egypt. Yet "Fayyum" persists as a title for the genre, in part because it was one of the first labels, but also, I suggest, because it carries with it a hint of the exotic, the "Egyptian," when conceived as entirely other.

British Museum in London mounted the program "Ancient Faces: Mummy Portraits from Ancient Egypt" from March 14 to July 20, 1998. Reviewers called the show, with its almost eighty portraits, a "huge success."[15] The method of display was important; objects were shown in darkened galleries, at human height, off the walls and seemingly standing in the middle of space, so viewers could walk among them. The museum was lauded for bringing to its visitors the "eye-opening splendor of some of antiquity's most ravishingly naturalistic images, displayed in glowing spot-lit darkness to dazzling effect."[16] Three years later, in 2000, an expanded version of the program went to the Metropolitan Museum of Art in New York City.[17] There, too, the aim was to grant visitors access to antiquity through the experience of touring the galleries. To that end, the exhibits also displayed other materials from the ancient world, highlighting the culture of Roman Egypt from between roughly 100 CE, the likely date of the first painting, and 500 CE, after which paintings of this style were no longer regularly made.

The effort made to contextualize the portraits within antiquity, though, can index for us just how far removed they were from that original context. What was on display—these "ancient faces"—had indeed been painted during the later part of the

15. Montserrat, "'To make death beautiful,'" 19. "The huge success of *Ancient Faces* and its spin-off merchandising (notelets, key-rings, postcards, jigsaws, and so on) showed that in the late 1990s the Fayum portraits found a perfect cultural moment. Why should this be? Is it another example of *fin-de-siècle* angst, that in the dying century only something as dead as the 'ancient faces' of mummies can be revived? Or does the transcendent 'realism' the portraits seem to possess strike a deeper, narcissistic chord of self-recognition? Their 'humanity' can easily seem to bind ancient and modern individuals across the cultural and temporal gulfs which separate us. In this respect, mummy portraits are potent cultural capital."

16. Jaś Elsner, "'Ancient Faces' at the British Museum," *Apollo* (July 1997): 48.

17. See Walker, *Ancient Faces*, particularly the "Director's Foreward," 7.

Mummy with intact portrait attached, Metropolitan Museum of Art, Rogers Fund 1911. "Mummy with an Inserted Panel Portrait of a Youth," The Met, https://www.metmuseum.org/art/collection/search/547697. Wikimedia commons.

Roman occupation of Egypt, though they were not designed as—nor did they survive as—portraits. In their original context, the "faces" that drew so much attention from European and North American visitors were just one component of a much larger and more valuable funerary creation: the preserved mummy of a loved one, created at the expense of both time and materials, with the "face" likely painted at the end of the long process of preservation—probably the piece of the assembled object most quickly created, and certainly the cheapest, as it was executed in egg, water, honey, and wax on wood.[18] When they were whole,

---

18. The one scholar who has insisted, rightly, on this fact is Corcoran, who eschews the term "mummy portrait" and instead speaks of "portrait mummies," when the entire object remains intact to be known. See Corcoran and

these objects had functions and contexts of their own. Firstly, they were to preserve whole the bodies of the dead, and ultimately, to make them portable: these pieces were taken and given in pawn, circulating to guarantee the financial commitments of those they had left among the living.[19]

The process that created the Fayyum portraits as they are now encountered started with these larger assemblages and extracted what was seen as valuable, but that fact can at times be obscured by the way that scholars talk about the portraits' origins. Though the production of a Fayyum portrait involved cutting the painted face away from a full mummy, accounts often speak of the "discovery" or "rediscovery" of the portraits in the late nineteenth century, as if it were then that they were first "brought to light," as if they had been buried only to wait for us to find them.[20] The method for taking and producing the paintings was far less mysterious. An antiquities dealer from Vienna, Theodor Graf, started to buy paintings in 1887, all coming from near the village of Rubayat, and put them on the ancient artifacts market.[21] A large

---

Svoboda, *Herakleides*, esp. 18–20, and Corcoran, *Portrait Mummies from Roman Egypt (I-IV Centuries A.D.) with a Catalog of Portrait Mummies in Egyptian Museums*, Studies in Ancient Oriental Civilization 56 (University of Chicago Press, 1995). Cf. Fenton, "The Mummy's Secret," 15, on the assembled object.

19. Klaus Parlasca, "Introduzione," in *el-Fayyum, introduzione e schede di Klaus Parlasca, testi di Jacques-Edouard Berger, Rosario Pintaudi*, ed. Franco Maria Ricci, I segni dell'uomo 35 (Franco Maria Ricci, 1985), 19 colA.

20. For the expression "brought to light," see Suzanna M. Grant, "Two 'Fayum' Portraits," *Bulletin of the Art Institute of Chicago* 72 (November–December 1978): 2; for "discovery," see Bierbrier, "The Discovery of the Mummy Portraits," in Walker, *Ancient Faces*; for "rediscovery," see Alfred Bernhard-Walcher, "Theodor Graf und die Wiederentdeckung der Mumienporträts," in *Bilder aus dem Wüstensand: Mumienporträts aus dem Ägyptischen Museum Kairo*, ed. Wilfried Siepel (Skira, 1998), 27–36.

21. For narratives of Graf's career, I am relying on the following essays: Morris Bierbrier, "The Discovery of the Mummy Portraits," in Walker, *Ancient Faces*, 32–33; Euphrosyne Doxiadis, "The Necropolisis of Philadelphia:

group was sold to a dealer in Cairo, others were eventually sold to individuals and museums, and several Graf held until his death, after which they were sold by his heirs. Estimates are that "by the end of his life some 350 had passed through his hands."[22] All this is to say: the mode of production was business. Graf did not excavate, from what we know, nor did he work on preserving any find information. Instead, he *harvested* the faces from funerary objects, or paid for it to be done. Graf arranged for parts of his collection to be exhibited in London, Munich, Paris, Brussels, and New York.[23] Their display was amplified by several different media, including newspaper articles and exhibition catalogs.[24] In other words, Graf created value by defacing, deracinating, then hyping and exhibiting the pieces, thereby training a market for them.[25]

Er-Rubayat and 'Kerke,'" in *Mysterious Fayum Portraits*, 129–33; Corcoran and Svoboda, *Herakleides*, 18–19; Berger, "Alla scoperta del Fayyum," in Ricci, *el-Fayyum*, 23–57.

22. Doxiadis, "The Necropolises of Philadelphia," 129; and Bierbrier, "Discovery," 32.

23. Doxiadis, "The Necropolises of Philadelphia," 131; and Bierbrier, "Discovery," 32 (New York). Also, they were exhibited at the Chicago World's Fair, in 1893. Greg Given has suggested to me an intriguing echo to be found in Claudia Breger's history of the German appropriation of the bust of Nefertiti. See Breger, "The 'Berlin' Nefertiti Bust: Imperial Fantasies in Twentieth-Century German Archaeological Discourse," in *The Body of the Queen: Gender and Rule in the Courtly World, 1500–2000*, ed. Regina Schulte (Berghahn Books, 2006), 281–305.

24. Doxiadis (*Mysterious Fayum Portraits*) lists them: *Allgemeine Zeitung*, nos. 135–37, 180 (May 16, 17, 18, and June 30): 1888; Otto Donner von Richter, *Die enkaustische Malerei der Alter* (Berlin, 1889); F. H. Richer et al., *Katalog zu Theodor Graf's Gallerie antiker Portraits aus hellenistischer Zeit* (Berlin, 1889); and R. L. C. Virchow, *Portrait-Muenzen und Graf's hellenistische Portrait-Galerie* (Berlin, 1902).

25. He also attempted to have all of them dated to the Ptolemaic period, ostensibly to have them go for higher values. See Doxiadis, "The Necropolises of Philadelphia," 132–33. While what the Egyptians did with their dead may

What is more, Graf inspired a kind of franchise that would visit other villages, too. While most of the portraits that Graf sold came from Rubayat, other sellers repeated the process in other places. Flinders Petrie worked in Hawara, sponsored by antiquities collectors.[26] He was better at documentation but brought the portraits north for exhibition, and continued to return to Egypt for thirty more years of attempts at extraction, starting in 1888 and continuing periodically through the 1910–11 excavation season. (We will return to his motives for this long work in a moment). Albert-Jean Gayet had pursued a similar strategy in Antinopolis, which involved excavating and selling to collectors—a "necessary evil," as he put it. His work resulted in exhibitions and volumes, the fruit of having opened "around ten thousand graves."[27]

We might wonder why these men became so interested in the harvesting of faces, when previously the painted placards on mummies had gone ignored for centuries. The first documented European knowledge of them comes from Pietro delle Valle, who

---

seem to us bizarre, what we have done with them can only be described as ghoulish.

26. Doxiadis, "The Necropolises of Philadelphia," 136. Cf. Paul C. Roberts, "'One of Our Mummies Is Missing': Evaluating Petrie's Records from Hawara," in *Portraits and Masks: Burial Customs in Roman Egypt*, ed. M. L. Bierbrier (British Museum Press, 1997), 19–25. Petrie's journals are, to put it mildly, one hell of a read. They are being transcribed online by the Griffith Institute, University of Oxford, http://griffith.ox.ac.uk.

27. Doxiadis, "The Necropolises of Antinopolis," in Doxiadis, *Mysterious Fayum Portraits*, 150, 152. The habit of harvesting from the dead for collecting purposes has a long and shameful history. See, for example, the history of Ales Hrdlicka's work in Nicole Duncga and Claire Healey, "Revealing the Smithsonian's 'Racial Brain Collection'," *Washington Post*, August 20, 2023. On the white practice of collecting Edgefield face vessels, see Adrienne Spinozzi, "Confronting, Collecting, and Celebrating Edgefield Stoneware," in *Hear Me Now: The Black Potters of Old Edgefield, South Carolina*, ed. Adrienne Spinozzi (Yale University Press, 2022), 39.

encountered some in 1615 and wrote about them in his journals published in the mid-seventeenth century.[28] As excavation of Egypt began in the 1800s, Moses Bierbrier wrote, "A trickle of portraits and portrait shrouds from Saqqara and probably Thebes, entered European collections . . . but failed to attract much attention."[29] That is to be expected, at some level, because what is extracted from a colony for consumption tends to change over time to match the desires of the age.[30] At the time, other extractions from the dead of Egypt were far more popular with European consumers. There was the pigment "mummy brown," for example, made by suspending ground powder from mummified corpses in a substrate for painting; it was in high demand during delle Valle's life, during the sixteenth and seventeenth centuries.[31] Before that, the most popular extract from mummies was *mumiya*, a medical preparation for ingestion similarly made from ground mummy powder. Europeans especially coveted it from the 1400s through the 1600s, in part because of the desire for exotic preparations and spices, if not from the New World and Asia, then from the oldest of worlds, Egypt.[32] Egypt had for centuries seemed to its neighbors to the north a bounty of

---

28. Bierbrier, "Discovery," 32.

29. Bierbrier, "Discovery," 32.

30. Berger predicted this without appending the history of changing habits of consumption: "If the Fayum portraits had been unearthed earlier, during, say, the eighteenth century, they would, I believe, have been considered as little more than a curiosity . . . these little paintings on linen or wood would probably have seemed diffident, clumsy, cursory, repetitive, uninspired" ("Fayum Portrait Painters," in Berger, *Portraits*, 10–11).

31. Anne Godfraind-De Becker, "Utilisations des momies de l'antiquité à l'aube du xxᵉ siècle," *Revue des questions scientifiques* 181 (2010): 306–40.

32. See the entries for *athanasia* and *pillule Gallicae* in Juhani Norri, *Dictionary of Medical Vocabulary in English, 1375–1550: Body Parts, Sicknesses, Instruments, and Medical Preparations* (Routledge, 2016). I am grateful to Stephanie Yoon for helping me locate this resource. Cf. Butter London's

resources, a place that "has always had new treasures to bestow," and the harvested faces that we call "portraits" are just the latest in products extracted, taken, then marketed.[33]

But nineteenth-century European men on the hunt for treasures did not want a medical powder or a base for a particular paint color. What was most salient, most valuable, to them was the face, or at least the appearance of one. That is why excavators separated the painted placards from the bodies that they had been made to accompany, rummaging through grave after grave (recall Gayet's estimate: approximately ten thousand!) and slicing away the desired part, leaving behind the carefully preserved bodies of ancient people to get at the representation they cherished. Beyond engaging in the physical labor of extracting faces, excavators also did more, often retouching or fully repainting what they had taken to resemble more closely a portrait of a face. James Fenton relates a long story about how Flinders Petrie melted the wax of a painting by holding it over a candle, then made corrections to the image to make it seem more real, more arresting.[34] Production of faces was so central to the whole enterprise that pastiches were created to mimic whole portraits, pulled together from the remains of anywhere from two to a half-dozen other seemingly "incomplete" faces.[35] In this

---

"Yummy Mummy" nail polish—a taupe-y brown, and surely a reference to the color of mummy brown, alongside a play on words for sexy mothers.

33. Berger, "Alla scoperta," in Ricci, *el-Fayyum*, 27 colA: "L'Egitto ha sempre nuovi tesori da elargire."

34. Fenton, "The Mummy's Secret"; cf. Doxiadis, *Mysterious Fayum Portraits*, 146.

35. The Toledo Museum of Art held a pastiche (1906.172) in its permanent collections from 1906 until 1991, when it was decommissioned and eventually sold at Sotheby's (personal communication with Alison L. Huftalen, October 2021). See also D. L. Thompson, "A Patchwork Fayum in Toledo," *American Journal of Archaeology*, 77 (1973): 438–39; Graham Weber, "Giving the Dead Their

way, excavators and dealers could extract every possible bit of value from their takings.[36]

The drive to find and produce portraits for consumption is comprehensible, given what meaning individual faces had taken on in the late 1800s. Since antiquity, the genre of the painted portrait has captured human attention, particularly for its ability to represent likeness. But ever since the invention of light-based photography in 1839, photographs have overtaken portraits as a record of individuals and their faces. Because it is created from the light reflected from an object, a photograph can seem like a neutral medium, positivistic in its recording of just what is there. Holding a photograph of a person suggests that there was, at some time, a person who had posed for the photograph to be taken. It is an artistic and documentary medium that may be mundane now—how many pictures of yourself are you carrying in your pocket at this moment, let alone pictures of other people?—but at its inception, photography was practically magical. By creating a legible artifact of a person, the technology also inspired a theory of presence and essence. Photography *can* play tricks, of course, but the biggest trick it has played is granting a sense that it could capture real life and that, consequently, real life was a thing that could be captured, independent of a viewer's cultural training, and then passed along to other viewers to see it the same way.

Almost immediately after its invention, photography also meant more. As Sarah Blackwood explains, the decades after

---

Due: An Exhibition Re-Examines Funerary Portraits from Roman Egypt," December 21, 2022, https://harvardartmuseums.org/article/giving-the-dead-their-due-an-exhibition-re-examines-funerary-portraits-from-roman-egypt. This details the pastiche numbered #12413 and describes its acquisition.

36. Because of the assembly of so many pastiches, Elsner raises the potential for fakery, something he criticizes the British Museum exhibit for not explicitly addressing. See "'Ancient Faces,'" 49.

the invention of photography saw photographers and consumers of photography alike likening the medium to portraiture, as both were able to capture something peculiar to their subjects; the ideals of physical representation tracked with newly articulated theories of human psychology.[37] An early history of photography, written just before the end of the American Civil War, made the peculiarities of each subject central. Marcus Aurelius Root reflected,

> I have repeatedly and most emphatically urged that expression is *essential* to a portrait, whether taken with a camel's hair pencil, or with the pencil of the sun. Nor can this point be pressed too often or too forcibly, For a portrait, so styled, however splendidly colored, and however skillfully finished its manifold accessories, is worse than worthless if the pictured face does not show the *soul* of the original—that *individuality* or *selfhood*, which differences *him* from all beings, past, present, or future.[38]

That individuality is, to some extent, what drives the current fascination with the Fayyum portraits.

These products of the nineteenth century suggest to us that we might, through them, have a connection to individuals from antiquity, a connection that is exquisitely difficult to establish through most other historical records from the distant past. Ancient evidence about humanity tends to represent only the wealthiest and most select parts of a society, with the stories and experiences of the vast majority of individuals absolutely inaccessible. This lack of sources imposes great difficulty on imagining the variety of

---

37. Sarah Blackwood, *The Portrait's Subject: Inventing Inner Life in the Nineteenth Century United States* (University of North Carolina Press, 2019).

38. Marcus Aurelius Root, *The Camera and the Pencil, or the Heliographic Art* (Lippencott, 1864), 143, cited by Blackwood, *The Portrait's Subject*, 3 (emphasis in original, i.e., in Root, and reproduced by Blackwood).

individual lives during the period, though scholars have certainly tried.[39] Scholarly books currently in circulation that discuss identity or the self bear Fayyum portraits on their covers, a signal that gazing on their faces might somehow allow us to reach that most elusive of targets—a particular, single, human experience.[40]

There is even a sense that the portraits, following the potential of photography, could bring otherwise inaccessible individuals to historical salience. Even when photography was at its most difficult, it was faster, easier, and cheaper than painting. As Blackwood notes, the earliest consumers of photography grasped this unusual feature. She reports Frederick Douglass giving a public lecture in 1861 in Boston, where he "celebrated photographic technology for its role in democratizing portraiture."[41] The affordability of photographs, in both the time and expense spent to create them, fostered their ubiquity. As Douglass observed, "Daguerreotypes, Ambrotypes, Photographs, and Electrotypes, good and bad, now adorn or disfigure all our dwellings. . . . Men of all conditions may see themselves as others see them. What was once the exclusive luxury of the rich and great is now within reach of all."[42] Thus, the medium of photography held out the promise

39. Jörg Rüpke, for example, has attempted to capture individuality and the processes of individuation. See Rüpke, *On Roman Religion: Lived Religion and the Individual in Ancient Rome* (Cornell University Press, 2016). See also Éric Rebillard and Jörg Rüpke, eds., *Group Identity and Religion Identity in Late Antiquity* (Catholic University of America Press, 2015).

40. See, for instance, the cover of Maia Kotrosits, *Rethinking Early Christian Identity: Affect, Violence, and Belonging* (Fortress, 2015) or that of David Brakke et al., eds., *Religion and the Self in Antiquity* (Indiana University Press, 2005).

41. Blackwood, *The Portrait's Subject*, 63. See also the observations of Naomi Miyazawa, "Poe, the Portrait, and the Daguerreotype: Poe's Living Dead and the Visual Arts," *Poe Studies* 50 (2017): 88–106.

42. Frederick Douglass, cited in Blackwood, 63, as "Lecture on Pictures"; however, as she notes, it was also printed as "Pictures and Progress: An

of being able to represent the average person—not the emperor, nor the king, nor the senator, but the boy, the girl, the city dweller, the worker, the farmer, the enslaved person. The Fayyum portraits, too, have been hailed as a resource by which to see a wide range of individuals from antiquity. Otherwise mostly unremarkable, the people in the portraits are very different from the usual subjects of representation that are seen in ancient art— they, too, are neither the emperor nor the king, but the nameless boy, the woman, the worker. The prospect that the Fayyum portraits might represent some average person and their characteristics was a factor in the impulse to create them in the first place.

II: A FAMILY ALBUM?

For dealers and excavators, the faces of the Fayyum portraits were the most valuable thing that could be gotten from Egyptian grave sites. That was in part, as we have seen, because the portraits held out the promise of connecting viewers to individuals from antiquity. Other logics also drove the production of the portraits, including the desire to bring to the surface something far more elusive, and collective, that might be represented in them: the existence of races among human beings and the history of their mixture or purity. W. M. Flinders Petrie, one of the collectors responsible for a fair number of portraits, was committed to proving the tenets of the nineteenth century's racial science.

To Petrie, the paintings represented a data trove from which he could extrapolate facial features important to race science, such as forehead size, nose shape, and facial slope. In his 1888

Address Delivered in Boston, Massachusetts, On December 3 1861" in *The Frederick Douglass Papers*, vol. 3, ed. John W. Blassingame (International, 1959), 452–73.

essay in *Nature* titled "The Earliest Racial Portraits," he made the case for using Fayyum portraits to show the distinction between races, even to trace the potential lineage of reproduction that created such distinction. Petrie explains his purposes at length:

> An interesting study of the mixture of races may be made from the coloured wax paintings of the Roman age which I discovered this year in the Fayum. From those we see how largely Greek and Italian blood penetrated into Egypt far inland, and how it became mixed with the native race; showing that the Copt, though pure from Arab admixture since the Muhammedan conquest, is far from being of a pure race. We have therefore in the Copts a most interesting example for study; as the effect of climate in unifying a heterogeneous mixture, and subduing elements foreign to the country, can be here observed without any admixture of fresh races for twelve hundred years. A thorough anatomical study of the average Copt in comparison with the elements of ancient Egyptian, Negro, Ethiopian, Arab, Greek, and Roman, would throw light on the great question of climate *versus* race in the causation of characteristics. We have a specimen race duly compounded, and then safely set apart for future examination, owing to the power of fanaticism, which has been an absolute barrier to future combinations.[43]

By Petrie's reasoning, a collection of portraits like his, when read with an eye to racially identified facial features, could tell the deep history of race purity and miscegenation in Egypt. Copts, presumably those represented in the portraits, are the result of Greek and Roman colonization in antiquity, a process that was to Petrie frozen in time by the advent of Islam; he imagined such a gulf between Christians and Muslims that the two groups would

---

43. W. M. Flinders Petrie, "The Earliest Racial Portraits," *Nature*, December 6, 1888, 128–30. As I described earlier, Petrie also "adjusted" the faces of the paintings he gathered, melting some of them over candles in order to make his corrections. See Doxiadis, *Mysterious Fayum Portraits*, 146.

remain genetically separate over centuries. Petrie was invested in how the portraits might evidence this history; he was also interested in how the climate of Egypt might blunt the expression of racially identified features. What is most important, Petrie was eager to share his tranche of portrait evidence with others; to him it is "unmuddled," documentary proof of both the races he projects onto the past and their interaction (or lack of interaction) with one another.

In this aspect, the discourse around the portraits again resonates with what had been thought possible in photography from its inception. Reading racial lineage—the essence of a depicted subject's stock and blood—in a face was one of photography's first widespread uses. Roland Barthes asserts its centrality to the genre, saying that photographs take a face and "manifest its genetic essence," revealing what might otherwise not be seen by the observer in the flesh.[44] In the earliest days of the technology, the practice of using photography to taxonomize human beings spanned registers from the academic to the domestic.

On the academic side, for instance, British theorist Francis Galton had already set out his ideas about race and racial hierarchy among humans in the middle of the nineteenth century.[45] But by the 1880s Galton had hit upon a way to prove his taxonomy. As Shawn Michelle Smith documents, Galton took multiple frontally posed mug shots of people, exposing the same piece of film to one face after another, until he reached what he called a composite, something to represent the average of the individuals captured

---

44. Barthes, *Camera Lucida*, 103. Cf. 105: What photographs show is "an identity stronger, more interesting, than legal status."

45. I draw my account of Galton's work from Shawn Michelle Smith, *American Archives: Gender, Race, and Class in Visual Culture* (Princeton University Press, 1999), 122–32.

on film. The magic of composition took away individual oddities and showed what was truly common among the photographed; it was for him a way to reveal their true nature. The qualities of the nature that Galton wanted to mark are striking: criminality, disease (especially tuberculosis), and Jewishness are the "types" that he said he had managed to capture with his technique.[46] Galton's composite images look, in fact, very much like the Fayyum portraits: they are contextless, frontally posed, placid of expression, seemingly individual and collective at the same time. What is more, photography like Galton's created in others the habit of interpretation, of racial scrying, that powered the creation of the portraits. As Smith argues, photographic activities like Galton's "generated and maintained essentialized discourses of interior character, and trained observers in how to read the body for the signs of a knowable interiority."[47] What was in a face was a life, as well as a lineage.

Equating photographed faces with familial lineage powered other industries related to photography. On the domestic side, the production and marketing of family albums, seemingly just sentimental archives, were tied up with the creation and valuation of whiteness.[48] It is telling, as Smith narrates, that alongside his criminal composites, Galton also produced a template for parents to use in this context, the "Life History Album." In it, parents could record the physical and developmental qualities of their children, picture by picture securing evidence of their fitness and good breeding.

---

46. Smith, *American Archives*, see figures on 88, 90, 164, as well as the discussion on 160–67.

47. Smith, *American Archives*, 4.

48. Smith, *American Archives*, esp. "'Baby's Picture Is Always Treasured': Eugenics and the Reproduction of Whiteness in the Family Photograph Album," 113–35.

Knowing this history of use for photography gives a different flavor to two relatively recent kinds of reception for the Fayyum portraits. First, consider the way that dissection and investigation of the portraits has followed the interpretive logic of early photographic technology. Faces in Galton's photography were read for signs of disease or for traces of lineage. Several attempts have been made to similarly read the Fayyum portraits in order to identify and diagnose disease. That interest, ironically, has returned significance to the previously unvalued mummified bodies that still bear some of the portraits. Suddenly, with scientific techniques like magnetic resonance imaging, the bodies that previously had been cast away were again legible, useful, and important to preserve. Identified by their paintings, bodies were scanned to reveal diseases and pathologies, some indicated by oddities of the face.[49] Art historians know, and tell others, that portraits are not scans to be used for diagnosis.[50] And yet, new photographic techniques inspired new examination and, with that examination, new defacement, a century after Europeans had harvested the paintings and gathered them into a genre of portraits.

Second, in the latter part of the twentieth century, these portraits were collected and published in lush coffee table books, which presented the individual images almost as if they were photographs collected in a precious album. Franco Maria Ricci presented *el-Fayyum* in an embossed black box, the cover resplendent with gold lettering and a glossy color portrait pasted to

---

49. Judith Barr et al., "The Girl with the Golden Wreath: Four Perspectives on a Mummy Portrait," *Arts* 8, no. 92 (2019): esp., part 4; O. Appenzeller et al., "Neurology in Ancient Faces," *Journal of Neurology, Neurosurgery, and Psychiatry* 70, no. 4 (2001).

50. Yael Rice and Sonja Drimmer, "How Scientists Use and Abuse Portraiture," *Hyperallergic*, December 11, 2020.

the hardboard (*Ritratto di Isidora*, a piece held by the J. Paul Getty Museum). The interior paper was light blue, pin-striped, and had the hefty weight of fine stationery. It bore more glossy tipped-in plates of the portraits, each with at least one corner free (presumably to emphasize the similarity to photographs pasted in to albums); the final pages were graced with a note about the book's limited print run, including a handwritten book number—to write this essay, I worked with book #141/5000.[51] Ricci's album was matched a decade later by a sleek book from Harry N. Abrams Publishers, *The Mysterious Fayum Portraits*, written by Euphrosyne Doxiadis. It, too, was produced at some expense, its glossy pages bearing images of the portraits that are even larger than Ricci's, some of them taking up the whole of the twelve-by-nine-inch space of the page. In these beautifully produced albums, ethnicity and lineage are central to the identifications applied to the portraits; by scanning the particular features of each, collectors had come to label a portrait as "the Jew" or "the European," labels that persist as captions to each portrait.[52]

If nineteenth-century families had created similar albums to show proof of their lineage, what do the albums of the Fayyum portraits point to?

III: ANOTHER FAMILY ALBUM?

Among the many tropes in the reception of the Fayyum portraits is the act of marveling, being struck by the portraits, their seeming

---

51. Ricci, *el-Fayyum*.

52. The traditional labels for some portraits are available in Ricci, *el-Fayyum*, while, overall, the portraits are said to have a "decidedly Oriental air" in Parlasca, "Introduzione," in Ricci, *el-Fayyum*, 19, 20. Graf originally presented all the portraits as "Greek." See the publicity poster for the 1894 Vienna exhibition in Corcoran and Svoboda, *Herakleides*, 19.

modernity, and feeling them to be either out of place or out of time. The natural next step is to wonder about their origin, which many viewers do. But, for the answer, viewers are not usually looking for something like the history of production I narrated above. Pulled by the logic of faces and what faces might be able to show, more often the direction that their wonder takes is toward lineage—much like the collation of faces in the photographic archives of the nineteenth century, but also along the lines, in ancient terms, of *origo*.[53] These faces, unexpected as they are, draw forth a question often asked of people who are deemed striking or unexpected: "What are you doing here?" but couched in a different, more invasive way—namely, "Where are you from?"

As the portraits themselves refuse to answer the question, interpreters must guess, and the pattern of guessing visibly hinges on ideas about parentage, lineage, and even breeding. The answer to that question *could* be very simple. The paintings were, as we have learned, taken from Egypt, through processes intent on their extraction, and consequently many of them are not attached to extensive find site information or other contextualizing details. Many have arrived to us with no known provenance. Still, we do retain a basic knowledge of where the majority were produced: in the villages of Upper Egypt, places like Memphis, Saqqara, Arsinoe, and the general area known as the Fayyum, for which the genre has been named.[54] The styles of painting vary, as

---

53. See Susanna Elm, "The Human Condition: *Condicio* and *origo* in Augustine (Letters 10*, 20*, and 24*)," in *Making Sense of the Oath*, ed. Stephan Esders, Cultural Encounters (Brepols, *forthcoming*); "Sold to Sin through *origo*: Augustine of Hippo on Slavery and Freedom," *Studia Patristica* 98 (2017): 1–21; and her forthcoming monograph, *Sold: Augustine of Hippo on Slavery, Taxation, and Original Sin*.

54. Doxiadis (*Mysterious Fayum Portraits*) covers specific provenances and those paintings that are unprovenanced. See section III: The Find Sites, 122–84. Cf. Walker, *Ancient Faces*, 38–119; Parlasca, *Mumienportraits*.

do the methods, but the basic answer is that these paintings come from villages in Egypt.

In scholarship about the paintings, though, the answer has not been so simple, much like the question "Where are you from?" is never really satisfied by the simple answer. This is in part because the political history of Egypt has been imprinted on the way scholars think about the artistic work the paintings represent. The Egypt that produced the portraits was politically a colony, and had been for at least hundreds of years by the time of the painting of the earliest extant portrait.

Locating the portraits within this history leads scholars to make some extremely complex proclamations about their origins. Because they were produced during the time of colonial domination of Egypt, they are not reckoned to be simply or merely Egyptian. Instead, they are the progeny of Egypt and its various colonizers. At times, the contributors to the creation of the paintings are two, and they are chronologically arranged: Egypt before its colonization and Rome (or before that, Greece) after colonization—as if at colonization, native responsibility for cultural production completely ceases. Exemplary in this vein is John Taylor's assessment: "The mummy portraits of Roman Egypt were the product of two traditions, that of Pharaonic Egypt and that of the Classical world."[55] In this scheme, contemporary Roman

---

55. John Taylor, "Before the Portraits: Burial Practices in Pharaonic Egypt," in Walker, *Ancient Faces*, 9. The pattern of naming these two entities as forbears crosses a very wide range of writing about the portraits. See, for other examples, Jaś Elsner, "'Ancient Faces'"; Elisabeth R. O'Connell, "Fayyum Portraits," in *Oxford Dictionary of Late Antiquity*, ed. Oliver Nicholson (Oxford University Press, 2018); Christina Riggs, *The Beautiful Burial in Roman Egypt: Art, Identity, and Funerary Religion* (Oxford University Press, 2006), particularly the discussion from 136 to 173.

Egypt—which is to say, the Egypt where the paintings were made and lived until excavators claimed them—plays no role.

Other accounts of the portraits' origins assume these two contributors, then assign judgments about the relative worth of the contributions of each. Kurt Gschwantler, for instance, comments that "the mummy portraits of Roman Egypt came into being as the result of two traditions." This comes followed by an analysis of the components: "In style and technique they are the product of Greco-Roman portrait painting, though in functionality they are integral to the preparation of mummies in the last phase of the Egyptian cult of the dead."[56] The separation of the methods is subtle in Dorothy J. Thompson's observation that "In these painted portraits the traditions of Greece become joined to ancient Egyptian practices."[57] And it is still just under the surface in Euphrosyne Doxiadis's summation that the objects are the result of the Greek painting tradition uniting with the Egyptian commitment to the immortal. She characterizes this phenomenon as follows: "Of these two strands, the sophistication of the first and the intensity of the second combined to produce moments of breathtaking beauty and unsettling presence in the paintings that survive."[58]

Greek sophistication, Egyptian intensity. A variation on this pattern sees not two but three contributors to the creation of the

56. Kurt Gschwantler, "Graeco-Roman Portraiture," in Walker, *Ancient Faces*, 21.

57. Doxiadis, forward to *Mysterious Fayum Portraits*, 11.

58. Doxiadis, "Technique," in Walker, *Ancient Faces*, 30. See also Campbell C. Edgar, "On the Dating of the Fayum Portraits," *Journal of Hellenic Studies* 25 (1905): 225–33, which has a description that almost takes on the character of a breeding report: "The early masks are tentative essays in an alien art, the style of the paintings from the beginning is free and finished and entirely Greek" (231). Riggs (*Beautiful Burial*) also describes portraiture as an art "alien" to Egyptians (96, 173).

objects, as in the case of Phillipe Montebello: "powerful promise of the Egyptian afterlife, the pervasiveness and coherence of Roman culture and the strong naturalism of the Graeco-Roman painting tradition" combine to create the portraits.[59] Egyptian afterlife, Roman culture, Greek tradition. The pattern shows in higher relief in other critics' work, such as Susan Walker's note that the genre is the result of a "remarkable coexistence of . . . Greek cultural heritage . . . Roman domination of the political and social order . . . and the Egyptian way of dealing with the dead."[60] That "way" is something, Walker says, that must have seemed "bizarre" to the Romans who conquered Egypt. These pronouncements all credit at least two cultures for the portraits—Greek and Egyptian, or Greek-via-Roman and Egyptian—but make clear the value of the contribution of each. The colonizing culture provides the tradition and its "sophistication," while the colonized provides the cult and its "bizarre" "intensity."[61]

There is, of course, no rule that any genre of art must be explained by or located in a lineage or parentage. Reproduction is not the only framework for cultural production. There are other ways to contextualize cultural products, but these combinative explanations recur in almost every discussion of the paintings. To date, I have yet to find one that *does not* make this kind of statement. There is always a pairing—someone, if not older then wiser

---

59. Walker, *Ancient Faces*, 7.

60. Walker, *Ancient Faces*, 25.

61. This way of thinking can even create zombie art, as when Susan Walker speaks of "the latter type of Roman portrait [funerary portraits] that found its way to Egypt" as if a type of art could just wander off (23). This awareness of funerary portraiture is double-edged: if it was Roman, how "bizarre" and "Egyptian" could it be when practiced in Egypt? For more on portraits in funerary contexts, see Grace Stafford, "Between the Living and the Dead: Use, Reuse, and Imitation of Painted Portraits in Late Antiquity," *Journal of Roman Archaeology* 35 (2022): 683–712.

than Egypt—telling her what to do, introducing art and sophistication to her "bizarre" little cultural obsession with the dead. With that comment I jokingly draw a comparison to the budding romance in *The Sound of Music*, but the description is accurate. These paintings, these people, are imagined as the result of a genealogy, a recombination of traits in which one is dominant, lending its long-acquired technical prowess to the undisciplined other. At least a few of the reckonings become quite literal, explaining that colonizer men married Egyptian women, and that is what brought about the art we see. (One wonders where the Egyptian men of the time would have gone).[62] Thus, the genre of the Fayyum portrait is the child of this cultural relationship between Egypt and her colonizer.

Of course, that means that the actual makers—first- to fourth-century people, living in Egypt, making these objects as part of larger funerary assemblages—are again elided. Instead, we are presented with a biological process slightly askew. It is the correct parentage, an unbroken lineage of Greek or Roman or Greco-Roman, combining with traditions thought to lack the refinement and skill available in the portraiture of a so-called classical nature. No one puts it quite as starkly as John Berger, who labels the portraits "a hybrid, totally bastard art-form," but the undertones are consistently there.[63] His vulgarity brings into undeniable relief the larger reproductive and cultural logics at work. If the genre of the portraits is a child, and its parents are

---

62. For instance, see John Ray, "On the Way to Osiris," *Times Literary Supplement*, September 27, 1996, 36, cited by Montserrat, "'To make death beautiful'," 4. Even the Wikipedia article on Fayyum portraits makes this point. See Wikipedia, "Fayum Mummy Portraits," last updated May 2, 2025, 16:44 (UTC), https://en.wikipedia.org/wiki/Fayum_mummy_portraits.

63. Berger, "Fayum Portrait Painters," in Berger, *Portraits*, 7.

Egypt and the Greek or Roman culture that colonized Egypt, the portraits secure a different kind of ancestry. As a result, the portraits are roundly acclaimed, with few exceptions, as "the only surviving examples of antique portrait painting."[64]

Now, physical evidence suggests that Greek and Roman cultures were keen, in fact, to represent the human being, in sculpture, on coins, on carved gems. Of course, usually these representations are of high-status individuals, such as emperors or mythical characters. On the basis of those, a scholar can say that portraiture is "one of the most successful and enduring genres of Roman art."[65] And yet, actual paintings, on surfaces, of individuals are vanishingly few in antiquity. Several small pieces exist, but those that have focus on a face are rare—the couple in Terentius Neo's house in Pompeii are the closest in execution, these from southern Italy—and the rest tend to be full-body representations.[66] So much for the physical evidence.

Textual evidence, however, can be found in descriptions of artistic practices. Because there are very few specimens of Greek or Roman portrait painting, the existence of a tradition of portraiture—individualized, highly varied, naturalistic—is frequently derived from Pliny the Elder's description of painting practices in (mostly) book 35 of his *Natural History*; published in 77

---

64. Kurt Gschwantler, "Graeco-Roman Portraiture," in Walker, *Ancient Faces*, 14: "And they are accordingly of great value. Virtually all Graeco-Roman panel painting has been lost . . ." Cf. Maria Nowicka, *Le portrait dans la peinture antique* (Academia Scientiarum Polona, 1993), particularly the forward; and Paolo Liverani, "I ritratti dipinto in età tardoantica," in *Figurationen des Porträts*, ed. Thierry Greub and Martin Roussel (Fink/Brill, 2018), 295–327.

65. Walker, *Ancient Faces*, 23.

66. The prospect of still other portraits, particularly in use in catacomb burials, is deftly raised by Stafford, "Between the Living and the Dead."

CE, it discusses several artists active four hundred years earlier, in Greece rather than in southern Italy. Among them is Apelles, who stands out for his ability to "paint to life"; several anecdotes charm the reader while confirming his talent.[67] Using this narrative description, scholars take naturalism to be a feature of Greek portrait painting, based on what is described by a Roman writer. And yet, as Geschwantler and others lament, "virtually all Graeco-Roman panel painting has been lost."[68] In this way, the Fayyum portraits become invaluable as possible evidence, not of their own production and context but of the artful tradition that *must* have preceded them.

Euphrosyne Doxiadis is even more direct about the debt the genre owes, as the very vocabulary she chooses to employ appears to be semaphore: "The Fayum corpus of painted portraits is of paramount significance in the history of art because it embodies the great Greek painting tradition."[69] If we attend her choice of words, a more specific schema is revealed. It is the *corpus* of painted portraits from Egypt that *embodies* the tradition that Doxiadis clearly reveres. The presence of an Egyptian face, a material object conceived, likely paid for, and executed in the villages of Egypt—no, not one, but hundreds of objects like this—is the evidence for a *Greek* tradition, which, again, has no real presence of its own in the historical record (and only Pliny's questionable[?], centuries-later account of Apelles to vouch for it). That does not

---

67. Pliny, *Natural History* 35.36.79–97. There is the story about his painting left as a calling card for Protogenes, though that painting no longer existed, having burned in a fire, Pliny says; another story about how Apelles hangs out behind his exhibited paintings so he can hear what viewers say about his work; and one about how multiple painters try to depict horses, but they all do so badly that a real horse only neighs at Apelles' rendering of the animal.

68. Walker, *Ancient Faces*, 14.

69. Walker, *Ancient Faces*, 30.

stop, in this scenario, the Greek tradition from surpassing its own bastard child. Weirdly, the variety, charm, and specificity of the mummy portraits—which, again, are practically the only exempla!—are relegated to a supposed decline in the tradition they supposedly embody. Their execution is a devolution from the part of the tradition that "ancient sources tell us, reached its peak at the time of Apelles in the fourth century BC[E]."[70]

Thought of in this way, the portraits are a specimen that proves a family line that is in reality unrepresented in the material record. As a product of the union of Greek art and Egyptian cult, the mummy portraits must have gotten whatever they show of skill or sophistication from their father: the absent, unseen, conjectured Greco-Roman tradition. Though they always come with the caveat that they are Egyptian in function—*partus sequitur ventrem*—they are most valuable because they indicate the father, his work and his worth.[71] There is no reason that a person happening on this archive of portraiture from the ancient world for the first time, unschooled in the pre-set valuations that attend colonizer and colonized (whether in the ancient world or the modern one), would ever think to invent this parent, yet it is a part of every major account of the portraits.

The idea that the paintings must be the product of the colonizing tradition—even as they are the only evidence of that tradition—is so strong that it overrides other, more obvious logics. Consider this: When Euphrosyne Doxiadis comes to wonder about how the portraits should be categorized, she decides that, although the paintings are found in Egypt, in funerary contexts, and although they represent people with Roman styling,

70. Doxiadis, "Technique," in Walker, *Ancient Faces*, 30.
71. Hortense J. Spillers, "Mama's Baby, Papa's Maybe: An American Grammar Book," *Diacritics* 17, no. 2 (1987): 64–81.

"the best of the portraits are still purely Greek."[72] To support this slightly idiosyncratic conclusion, Doxiadis tells a story about her mentor, "the great modern Greek painter" Yannis Tsarouchis, who lived from 1919 to 1989. When discussing the mummy portraits, the question of their provenance came up, and Doxiadis tells us that Tsarouchis said "that to regard the Fayum portraits as Roman is as absurd as saying that all the works he [Tsarouchis] created during the German occupation of Athens were German paintings."[73] Tsarouchis, who was dedicated to, as Doxiadis puts it, "record[ing] what was most deeply Greek" and "injecting vitality into age-old forms," finds it laughable that anyone would call his paintings a part of the tradition of the occupiers.

It is left unsaid, but of course the work produced by Tsarouchis—a man who was born, lived, worked, and died in Athens—would have to be called Greek. Tsarouchis's canny remark is meant as the end of the argument; it appears at the end of the paragraph, and after it, Doxiadis offers no more comments, but moves on as though the problem were solved. The logic of that story, though, does not transfer to Doxiadis's conclusion. The same story, told about a painter who was born, lived, worked, and died in the Fayyum, would require that that person's work be identified not with the culture of the current colonizer, nor that of the long-ago colonizer (in this case, Greece), but as Egyptian.[74]

---

72. Montserrat comments on how weird this is in "'To Make Death Beautiful'" (n4), where he also reports that Ray ("On the Way to Osiris") remarks on it.

73. Doxiadis, *Mysterious Fayum Portraits*, 12.

74. The equivalent to Doxiadis's argument would be claiming that Margaret Atwood, born in Ottawa in 1939 and resident in Toronto while writing, was a French novelist, because her areas of Canada had been colonized by France as late as 1763.

In all this lineage logic, there is a very strange toggling back-and-forth about what kind of material can be evidence for what kind of claim. What does any one piece of evidence from antiquity show us? Where can it be extrapolated and where can it not? As we have seen, the portraits are *not* Egyptian when it comes time to demonstrate the existence of a Greek or Roman painting tradition. And yet, they *are* Egyptian, subtly, when they are used in the contemporary world in a new context. Art historians have called for the portraits to be used to "diversify" the teaching of ancient art by expanding the range of subjects represented beyond the canon of European art.[75] As historians of the ancient world have come to terms with the whiteness of their perspectives on the past, they have sought to find and represent more diversity from the materials of the past. The portraits fulfill that: many have phenotypical features that modern people read as Blackness, and thus appear in the equivalent of college diversity brochures, there to represent in a conference or a program a demographic that may not be available to represent in actual photographs.

There are many examples, but I will start at home: the University of Michigan's Interdepartmental Program in Ancient History frequently uses a collocation of images of mummy portraits. One face—produced and reproduced, overlaid with (even more) color, washed in acid pink and green, Warhol-style—appears on the home page of the program and on the cover of our graduate student handbook. Other portraits appear in a row of seven across the top of the website for "Our Voices: A Conference for Inclusive Classics Pedagogy." At least three course advertisements for a recent single academic year at the University of Michigan used

---

75. Judith Barr, et al. "The Girl with the Golden Wreath," part 4; Christina Chin, "Excavate the Fayum Mummy Portraits and Bury Ancient Egyptian Stereotypes," *Art Education* 74 (2021): 14–20.

a Fayyum portrait to suggest the ancient topics under study. In the academic world more broadly, they appear frequently on the covers of books, as Dominic Montserrat observed.[76] One adorns the front cover of Berger's collection of portrait essays. In estimations that look back to traditions of the classical past, the portraits are decidedly *not* Egyptian, but in representations that look forward, the portraits are there specifically *to be* Egyptian. How can they be both? The portraits seem as if they can provide evidence of many things, and that is not an inherent quality of theirs; rather, it is something that was created by design, and far more recently.

IV: WHY WONDER?

So, the Fayyum portraits have borne a remarkably wide range of historical interpretations about what they represent or what they can prove about the ancient world. On an emotional level, the response they predictably induce, time after time, is wonder. Critics frequently place the portraits outside the realm of regular objects, insisting that their meaning lies beyond our understanding. For someone like Jean-Christophe Bailly, they are familiar, yet they "reside in a neutral place, neither death nor life . . . absolutely suspended."[77] While to some it can be "easy to imagine one knows" what they are, for others, no amount of thought or

---

76. Montserrat, "'To make death beautiful,'" n2. Cf. the books I have mentioned already (Kotrosits, *Identity*; Brakke et al., *Self*). Cf. also Sara Parks et al., *Jewish and Christian Women in the Ancient Mediterranean* (Routledge, 2021). Anna Lucille Boozer's *At Home in Roman Egypt: A Social Archaeology* (Cambridge University Press, 2021) might be the one book that can make a case for including the portrait on its cover, as it comes from the very context the book seeks to examine.

77. Bailly, *L'apostrophe muette*, 11. Indeed, Bailly's whole essay is like this in tone: wondrous and stunned.

contextualization will help, because the portraits bear "a secret no academic can unlock."[78] The mystery stems in part from their similarity to photography: what Barthes observes about photographs is also true here—they "utter interiority without yielding intimacy."[79] Or it is in part because they do not utter a thing. They seem to make a silent address, but remain mute, no matter how long we look.[80] They intrigue because they are as silent as the sphinx and as much of a riddle.[81]

Riddles are mechanisms that balance familiarity with mystery: the quotidian object described in a puzzling way, the unknown speaker who self-narrates then has to ask *us*, "Who am I?" Riddles are carefully constructed to sustain an equilibrium between knowing and not knowing; even when you know an answer to a riddle, you continue to thumb the feeling of not knowing, returning back to your ignorance, feeling the sense of revelation. The riddle rests in that epistemological balance, and the portraits follow a similar pattern. The pattern is not a matter of a question and an answer, but of realist style and very little context.

Despite the mystical air granted to them, the portraits are still just painted objects, coloration on a flat surface. Though their realism as a style makes it appear that there is a strong connection to individuals, we cannot know that any portrait represents any particular human being from antiquity.[82] It can seem like

78. The phrase, "easy to know," is from John Ray, "On the Way to Osiris"; "no academic" is from Doxiadis, *Mysterious Fayum Portraits*, 13.

79. Barthes, *Camera Lucida*, 98.

80. Berger, "Fayum Portrait Painters," in Berger, *Portraits*, 11; cf. Bailly: these faces do not say anything (136).

81. Berger ("Fayum Portrait Painters," in Berger, *Portraits*, 7) explicitly calls them a riddle.

82. Cf. Stephen Perkinson, *The Likeness of the King: A Prehistory of Portraiture in Late Medieval France* (University of Chicago Press, 2009).

they do, but paintings are ultimately *not* photography—as Barthes points out, "painting can feign reality without having witnessed it."[83] Portrait painters have long made use of this trick: realism can signal reality with absolutely no referent. As a style, it can be adopted at different times for different reasons. Consider Rembrandt, one of the most skillful artists of the period of high portraiture, said to be a master at capturing the essence of people. Rembrandt did paint historical people, but he also painted what are called "tronies," extremely realistic and individualized "portraits" of imagined people with no referent in reality. His imagination in painting them centered on odd headwear: Rembrandt created tronies for *The Old Man with the Turban, A Man with a Feathered Beret, An Old Man in Military Costume,* and *A Boy with an Elaborate Necklace*. None of these people actually existed, but they are painted in the same style as portraits for the living. Other artists also created characters, the most famous being Johannes Vermeer's *Girl with a Pearl Earring*.[84] Neither she nor the earring ever existed, though she seems real. Vermeer, like Rembrandt, used all of the methods of painting from life, but with none of the historical reference, thereby emptying out portraiture's implicit promise. Put shortly, realism in portraits is a style, not an epistemological bedrock.[85]

Realism certainly had a place in ancient art, but there, too, it is no guarantee of documentary. In ancient sculpture, there are

---

83. Barthes, *Camera Lucida*, 76.

84. Notice the echo in the article title in Judith Barr et al., "The Girl with the Golden Wreath."

85. Stafford, "The Living and the Dead," 690–91. The same goes for textual realism. See my reading of the realistic "diary" of Perpetua in Ellen Muehlberger, "Perpetual Adjustment: The *Passion of Perpetua and Felicity* and the Entailments of Authenticity," *Journal of Early Christian Studies* 30 (2022): 313–42.

realistic works, amazing for their ability to capture human form, but based on mythical figures. And, of course, what counts as realistic can vary widely. Often, ancient art stylized its representation of human beings. Even among the famously realistic Fayyum portraits, there is stylization—the portraits lack a sitting background and seem to come from nowhere. Recent analysis demonstrates a "strong underlying format to the paintings that deviates from the shape of human faces."[86] And, whatever style they express, the Fayyum portraits that remain connected to the mummy they were made for do not necessarily even match the body inside, which is, after all, no longer a living person.[87] In a Fayyum portrait, we are not guaranteed to meet the face of a real person, even when a person is being depicted—that face, or that which used to be a face, is in with the mummy.

Perhaps even more surprising, the prevailing theory about how style might influence viewing and reception suggests that we should *not* find ourselves fascinated by the Fayyum portraits, precisely *because* they are so detailed, so individualized, so real in appearance. To understand this theory, let me recount for you something of how modern comic drawing works. In cartoons, the effect of a realistic style on viewers' reception is quite

---

86. Jean Thistlewood et al., "Study of the Relative Locations of Facial Features within Mummy Portraits," in *Mummy Portraits of Roman Egypt: Emerging Research from the APPEAR Project*, ed. Marie Svoboda and Caroline R. Cartwright (Getty Museum, 2010), 10. Cf. Bob Brier and Caroline Wilkinson, "A Preliminary Study on the Accuracy of Mummy Portraits," *Zeitschrift für Ägyptische Sprache und Altertumskunde* 132 (2005): 107–11.

87. Fenton, "The Mummy's Secret," 14; Joyce M. Filer, "If the Face Fits . . . : A Comparison of Mummies and Their Accompanying Portraits Using Computerised Axial Tomography," in Bierbrier, *Portraits and Masks*, 121–26. I must note that when people think of the referent, they do not think of the mummy; they think of some ancient person somehow idealized, separate from the mummy and from the portrait, too.

pronounced. Artists have choices about the style they use to depict any given character, and, as Scott McCloud has explained, the more photorealistic the face of a character appears, the more a viewer will think of that character as a part of the world, external to herself. The less photorealistic (that is, the more "cartoony") a face is drawn, the more a reader is likely to imagine its experience as her own or, in short, to identify with that character. The practice of drawing the faces of certain characters with less detail than others in their surroundings is known as "masking," and cartoonists use it to induce a close affective response to characters whom they mask.[88]

The mummy portraits, however, are as real as can be and yet still draw audiences to identify with them, to wonder about them, to imagine how these objects from long ago might actually be about us, be speaking to us.[89] I suppose it is because these faces are still masked, just by a different technique: instead of lacking facial detail, most Fayyum portraits lack every other detail, like where, when, why, for whom, and how they were created. The process that made them removed them from their own context; the removal is crucial, as it is the taking away of the painted face from the body, and then that face out of the country, that allows

---

88. Scott McCloud, *Understanding Comics: The Invisible Art* (William Morrow, 1993), 92. For a very familiar example, consider the characters in Art Spiegelman's The Complete *Maus* (Pantheon, 1996): in historical scenes, Jews, drawn as mice, have the least detailed of faces, merely a triangle shape with dots for eyes and sometimes a line or two for a mouth; Germans in the same scenes, drawn as cats, have far more detailed faces, with whiskers, eyebrows, muzzles, and a fair amount of shading and crosshatching. An excellent place to see the difference is a scene (210), where a prisoner protests that he is actually not Jewish; Spiegelman draws the same character twice, in side-by-side panels, once as a mouse (and heavily masked in style) and once as a cat (still cartoonish but much less masked).

89. Bailly's entire project in *L'apostrophe muette*.

for wonder to bloom. We tell ourselves the paintings are universal, that they speak to us from nowhere. But that is because we have removed them from somewhere, where they were anything but universal; there, they were singular and embedded. The deracination creates a lack of knowledge without destroying the appearance of singularity. When devoid of the things that make an individual—life and context and kin and body—but not devoid of the signs of individual as a concept (namely, the face), the portrait is there for us to fill. Each of us is "spinning a history for a mute object," and with that history, creating for ourselves the delectable feeling of knowing based on one's reaction, rather than learning the actual context.[90]

What is more, lack of knowledge about the original circumstances of these portraits inspires only greater, not weaker, confidence—and thus speculation, which fills the gap, but only with improvisation, so that it can be performed over and over again with each new viewer. Thus, there is a balance of proximity and distance, proprietary feeling and mystery. Chronological distance and immediacy. Antiquity and modernity. These gaps do not, in general, cause viewers to change their assumptions about what the portraits represent, or to adjust their periodization of them or their estimation of what they evidence. Instead, they are led to cycles of wonder, then unknowing, then wonder. This is the "adventure" of the photograph that Barthes talks about.[91] It is also a version of the "adventure" that powers the study of the ancient world.[92] The gap that we perceive between our world and

---

90. Quotation from Smith, *American Archives*, 53.
91. *Camera Lucida*, 23.
92. Or, perhaps better, the thrill. See Andrew S. Jacobs, *Gospel Thrillers: Conspiracy, Fiction, and the Vulnerable Bible* (Cambridge University Press, 2023).

the ancient world is what allows us to imagine that we are creating new knowledge from old objects; it also assures us that there is more to be known, and it drives the impulse toward discovery. When knowing depends on not knowing, wonder is a manufactured response, and predictable.

ACKNOWLEDGMENTS

A book seems like a singular object, something that can and maybe should just stand on its own. In reality, though, a book is the thin, visible surface of a very deep well of conversations, the precipitate of drafts and revisions, difficulties, new investigations, and just plain effort, from its author, but also from many—so many!—others. Audiences at the University of Missouri, the University of Texas, the Canadian Society for Patristic Studies, and the community at the Boston Area Patristics Group all gave generative feedback to early versions of one or more of these essays. The community of fellows at the University of Michigan's Institute for the Humanities in 2021–22 shaped its development in ways that are hard to capture in words; I will always be grateful to them and to our wise leader, Peggy McCracken, for their good cheer and their challenge when we were all learning how to be together again in person. Jennifer Knust and the rest of the Late Ancient Studies Reading Group at Duke University graciously workshopped the whole manuscript, showing me where better interventions could be made.

Then there are the colleagues who stepped in to support or encourage or guide me as I worked. Jennifer Barry has been a constant friend and careful reader. When I was at sea with the lack of structure in the pandemic, she suggested we cowrite, and those virtual sessions have been a lifeline; now that Robin Whelan has joined us, our merry trio feels unstoppable. I am abundantly grateful to Susanna Elm, James O'Donnell, and Dan Sperber, who all championed my work to others. David Brakke has been helping me for a quarter century now, and for this book, he had excellent advice about publishers and audiences; it was through David that I got to meet Brad Storin, whose friendship and humor I treasure. Beth Digeser and Andrew Jacobs, both brilliant writers themselves, helped me see clearly what the project could be and what I needed to do to get it there. Colleagues in Ann Arbor like Christian de Pee and Michail Kitsos lent both their time and their good ideas, and Jonathan Farr's careful attention to the manuscript, bibliography, and index was invaluable. Last but not at all the least, I am grateful to Eric Schmidt, Jyoti Arvey, and Margo Irvin at the University of California Press, who all believed in this project and shepherded it with care.

And then, there are the people of my heart. When I started work on this book, we were four—my spouse, Gina Brandolino and I, and our two beloved cats, Tiny and Dodds. Now, as I finish it, the house is down to just two, and we are the least two—just the humans. Gina is my best reader, the person I count on for both encouragement and common sense. Tiny, a gloriously handsome, enormous tabby, broke all our hearts when he left us five years ago. Dodds lived on to be an eldercat, always dignified in his tuxedo yet eternally playful; he stayed with us until just a few weeks before I submitted this book. I thought about dedicating it to them both—they were the best of friends—but honestly, Tiny wasn't much of a reader. Dodds, though, was highly intelligent, hilarious, engaged with the humans around him in every way possible. He was such a faithful, sweet companion over the last five years that making this book for him was the obvious thing to do.

BIBLIOGRAPHY

ANCIENT SOURCES

Augustine of Hippo. *Confessions*. Edited by James J. O'Donnell. Clarendon, 1992.

Augustine of Hippo. *De fide et operibus*. In *Patrologiae cursus completus, series latina*. Vol. 40, edited by Jacques-Paul Migne. Paris, 1865.

Augustine of Hippo. *Enarrationes in Psalmos*. In *Patrologiae cursus completus, series latina*. Vol. 36, edited by Jacques-Paul Migne. Paris, 1858.

Cyril of Alexandria. *Cyril of Alexandria: Select Letters*. Edited and translated by Lionel R. Wickham. Clarendon, 1983.

DelCogliano, Mark, ed. and trans. *Christ: Chalcedon and Beyond*. Vol. 4, *The Cambridge Edition of Early Christian Writings*. Cambridge University Press, 2022.

DelCogliano, Mark, ed. and trans. *Christ: Through the Nestorian Controversy*. Vol. 3, *The Cambridge Edition of Early Christian Writings*. Cambridge University Press, 2022.

Eusebius of Caesarea. *Life of Constantine*. Translated by Averil Cameron and Stuart G. Hall. Clarendon Ancient History Series. Oxford University Press, 1999.

John of Ephesus. *The Third Part of the Ecclesiastical History of John Bishop of Ephesus*. Translated by R. Payne Smith. Oxford University Press, 1860.

Libanius. *Progymnasmata*. In *Libanii Opera* 8, edited by Richard Foerster. Teubner, 1915.

Life of St. Mary of Egypt. Translated by Maria Kouli. In *Holy Women of Byzantium: Ten Saints' Lives in English Translation*, edited by Alice-Mary Talbot. Dumbarton Oaks, 1996.

Mommsen, Theodore, and Paul M. Meyer, eds. *Theodosiani libri XVI cum Constitutionibus Sirmondianis et Leges novellae ad Theodosianum pertinentes*. Weidmanns, 1905.

Pharr, Clyde, ed. and trans. *The Theodosian Code and Novels, and the Sirmondian Constitutions*. In collaboration with Theresa Sherrer Davidson and Mary Brown Pharr. Princeton University Press, 1952.

Price, Richard, ed. and trans. *The Acts of the Council of Constantinople of 553, with Related Texts on the Three Chapters Controversy*. 2 vols. Translated Texts for Historians 51. Liverpool University Press, 2009.

Rufinus of Aquileia. *The Church History of Rufinus of Aquileia, Books 10 and 11*. Translated by Philip R. Amidon. Oxford University Press, 1997.

Severus Sophista Alexandrinus. *Severus Sophista Alexandrinus: Progymnasmata quae extant omnia*. Edited by Eugenio Amato. De Gruyter, 2009.

Shenoute of Atripe. *God Says Through Those Who Are His*. Edited and translated by Stephen Emmel. In *Selected Discourses of Shenoute the Great: Community, Theology, and Social Conflict in Late Antique Egypt*, edited by David Brakke and Andrew Crislip. Cambridge University Press, 2015.

Shenoute of Atripe. *Let Our Eyes*. Edited and translated by Stephen Emmel. In *Selected Discourses of Shenoute the Great: Community, Theology, and Social Conflict in Late Antique Egypt*, edited by David Brakke and Andrew Crislip. Cambridge University Press, 2015.

Shenoute of Atripe. *Not Because a Fox Barks*. Edited and translated by David Brakke and Andrew Crislip. In *Selected Discourses of Shenoute the Great: Community, Theology, and Social Conflict in Late Antique Egypt*, edited by David Brakke and Andrew Crislip. Cambridge University Press, 2015.

SECONDARY SOURCES

Amato, Eugenio, and Gianluca Ventrella. "L'éthopée dans la pratique scolaire et littéraire." In 'HΘOΠOIIA: *La représentation de caractères à l'époque impériale et tardive*, edited by Eugenio Amato and Jacques Schamp. Helios, 2005.

Ando, Clifford. "Pagan Apologetics and Christian Intolerance in the Ages of Themistius and Augustine." *Journal of Early Christian Studies* 4, no. 2 (1996): 171–207.

Appenzeller, O., J. M. Stevens, R. Kruszynski, and S. Walker. "Neurology in Ancient Faces." *Journal of Neurology, Neurosurgery, and Psychiatry* 70, no. 4 (2001): 524–29.

Azoulay, Ariella Aïsha. "Toward the Abolition of Photography's Imperial Rights." In *Capitalism and the Camera: Essays in Photography and Extraction*, edited by Kevin Coleman and Daniel James. Verso, 2021.

Bailly, Jean-Christophe. *L'apostrophe muette: Essai sur les portraits du Fayoum*. Hazan, 1997.

Barr, Judith, Clara M. ten Berge, Jan M. van Daal, and Branko F. van Oppen de Ruiter. "The Girl with the Golden Wreath: Four Perspectives on a Mummy Portrait." *Arts* 8, no. 3 (2019): 92.

Barry, Jennifer. *Bishops in Flight: Exile and Displacement in Late Antiquity*. University of California Press, 2019.

Barthes, Roland. *Camera Lucida: Reflections on Photography*. Translated by Richard Howard. Hill and Wang, 1981. Originally published as *La chambre claire: Note sur la photographie*. Editions de Seuil, 1980.

BeDuhn, Jason. *Augustine's Manichaean Dilemma*. Vol. 1, *Conversion and Apostasy, 373–388 C.E.* University of Pennsylvania Press, 2009.

Berger, John. "Alla scoperta del Fayyum." In Ricci, *el-Fayyum*.

Berger, John. "The Fayum Portrait Painters (1st–3rd century)." In *Portraits: John Berger on Artists*. Verso, 2015.

Bergjan, Silke-Petra, Bejamin Gleede, and Martin Heimgartner, eds. *Apollinarius und seine Folgen*. Studien und Texte zu Antike und Christentum 93. Mohr Siebeck, 2015.

Bernhard-Walcher, Alfred. "Theodor Graf und die Wiederentdeckung der Mumienporträts." In *Bilder aus dem Wüstensand: Mumienporträts aus dem Ägyptischen Museum Kairo*, edited by Wilfried Siepel. Skira, 1998.

Berzon, Todd S. *Classifying Christians: Ethnography, Heresy, and the Limits of Knowledge in Late Antiquity*. University of California Press, 2016.

Bierbrier, Morris. "The Discovery of the Mummy Portraits." In Walker, *Ancient Faces*.

Bierbrier, Morris (M. L.), ed. *Portraits and Masks: Burial Customs in Roman Egypt*. British Museum Press, 1997.

Blackwood, Sarah. *The Portrait's Subject: Inventing Inner Life in the Nineteenth-Century United States*. University of North Carolina Press, 2019.

Bond, Sarah E. *Trade and Taboo: Disreputable Professions in the Roman Mediterranean*. University of Michigan Press, 2016.

Boozer, Anna Lucille. *At Home in Roman Egypt: A Social Archaeology*. Cambridge University Press, 2021.

Borg, Barbara E. *"Der zierlichste Anblick der Welt": Ägyptischen Porträtmumien*. Philip von Zabern, 1998.

Borg, Barbara E. *Mumienporträts: Chronologie und Kultureller Kontext*. Philip von Zabern, 1996.

Borg, Barbara E. "Painted Funerary Portraits." In the *UCLA Encyclopedia of Egyptology*, edited by Willeke Wendrich, Jacco Dieleman, Elizabeth Frood, and John Baines. University of California, Los Angeles, 2010.

Bowes, Kimberly. "Inventing Ascetic Space: Houses, Monasteries and the Archaeology of Asceticism." In *Western Monasticism Ante Litteram: The Spaces of Monastic Observance in Late Antiquity and the Early Middle Ages*, edited by Henrik Dey and Elizabeth Fentress. Brepols, 2011.

Bowes, Kimberly. "Personal Devotions and Private Chapels." In *Late Ancient Christianity: A People's History of Christianity*, edited by Virginia Burrus. Fortress, 2005.

Brakke, David. *Demons and the Making of the Monk: Spiritual Combat in Early Christianity*. Harvard University Press, 2006.

Brakke, David. "Early Christian Lies and the Lying Liars Who Wrote Them: Bart Ehrman's *Forgery and Counterforgery*." *Journal of Religion* 96, no. 3 (2016): 378–90.

Brakke, David, Michael L. Satlow, and Steven Weitzman, eds. *Religion and the Self in Antiquity*. Indiana University Press, 2005.

Breger, Claudia. "The 'Berlin' Nefertiti Bust: Imperial Fantasies in Twentieth-Century German Archaeological Discourse." In *The Body of the Queen: Gender and Rule in the Courtly World, 1500–2000*, edited by Regina Schulte. Berghahn Books, 2006.

Brier, Bob, and Caroline Wilkinson. "A Preliminary Study on the Accuracy of Mummy Portraits." *Zeitschrift für Ägyptische Sprache und Altertumskunde* 132, no. 2 (2005): 107–11.

Brottier, Laurence. "Jean Chrysostome: Un pasteur face à des demi-chrétiens." *Topoi: Orient-Occident*, Supplement 5 (2004): 439–57.

Brown, Peter. *The Making of Late Antiquity*. Harvard University Press, 1978.

Brown, Peter. *Power and Persuasion in Late Antiquity: Towards a Christian Empire*. The Curti Lectures. University of Wisconsin Press, 1992.

Burr, Elizabeth G. "Libanius of Antioch in Relation to Christians and Christianity: The Evidence of Selected Letters." *Topoi: Orient-Occident*, Supplement 7 (2006): 63–76.

Buzi, Paolo. "*Codices Coptici Rescripti*: A Preliminary Census of the Palimpsests from the White Monastery." In *The Rediscovery of Shenoute: Studies in Honor of Stephen Emmel*, edited by Anne Boud'hours. Peeters, 2022.

Caseau, Béatrice. "Le crypto paganism et les frontières du licite: Un jeu de masques?" In *Pagans and Christians in the Roman Empire: The Breaking of a Dialogue (IVth–VIth Century A.D.)*, edited by Peter Brown and Rita Lizzi Testa. Lit, 2011.

Cassin, Matthieu. "Citer, collecter: Florilèges et citations d'auteurs patristiques dans les controverses doctrinales." Pts. 1 and 2. *Annuaire de l'EPHE, section des Sciences religieuses* 128 (2021): 217–29; 129 (2022): 271–83.

Chadwick, Henry. *Early Christian Thought and the Classical Tradition*. Clarendon, 1966.

Chin, Catherine M. "Apostles and Aristocrats." In Chin and Schroeder, *Melania*.

Chin, Catherine M., and Caroline T. Schroeder, eds. *Melania: Early Christianity Through the Life of One Family*. University of California Press, 2017.

Chin, Catherine M., and Moulie Vidas, eds. *Late Ancient Knowing: Explorations in Intellectual History.* University of California Press, 2015.

Chin, Christina. "Excavate the Fayum Mummy Portraits and Bury Ancient Egyptian Stereotypes." *Art Education* 74 (2021): 14–20.

Coleman, Kathleen M. "Portraits of Loss." In *Funerary Portraits from Roman Egypt: Facing Forward,* digital companion to the exhibition of the same title at Harvard Art Museums, August 27, 2022–December 30, 2022. https://harvardartmuseums.org/tour/770/slide/12400.

Corcoran, Lorelei H. *Portrait Mummies from Roman Egypt (I–IV Centuries A.D.) with a Catalog of Portrait Mummies in Egyptian Museums.* Studies in Ancient Oriental Civilization 56. University of Chicago Press, 1995.

Corcoran, Lorelei H., and Marie Svoboda. *Herakleides: A Portrait Mummy from Roman Egypt.* Getty Trust, 2010.

Daut, Winfried. "Die 'halben Christen' unter den Konvertiten und Gebildeten des 4. und 5. Jahrhunderts." *Zeitschrift für Missionswissenschaft und Religionswissenschaft* 55 (1971): 171–88.

De Montebello, Philipe. "Director's Foreword." In Walker, *Ancient Faces.*

De Vries, Wilhelm. *Orient et Occident: Les structures ecclésiales vues dans l'histoire des sept premiers conciles oecuméniques.* Cerf, 1974.

Dilley, Paul C. "The Invention of Christian Tradition: 'Apocrypha,' Imperial Policy, and Anti-Jewish Propaganda." *Greek, Roman, and Byzantine Studies* 50, no. 4 (2010): 586–615.

Donner von Richter, Otto. *Die enkaustische Malerei der Alten.* Berlin, 1889.

Douglas, Frederick. "Pictures and Progress: An Address Delivered in Boston, Massachusetts, on December 3, 1861." In *The Frederick Douglass Papers.* Vol. 3, edited by John W. Blassingame. International, 1959.

Dowlingsoka, Jo. "Refiguring Sex Work in the Life of Theodoros of Sykeon." *Studies in Late Antiquity* 6, no. 3 (2022): 457–81.

Doxiadis, Euphrosyne. *The Mysterious Fayum Portraits: Faces from Ancient Egypt.* Abrams, 1995.

Doxiadis, Euphrosyne. "Technique." In Walker, *Ancient Faces.*

Duncga, Nicole, and Claire Healey. "Revealing the Smithsonian's 'Racial Brain Collection'." *Washington Post,* August 20, 2023.

Durmaz, Reyham. *Stories Between Christianity and Islam: Saints, Memory, and Cultural Exchange in Late Antiquity and Beyond.* University of California Press, 2022.

Edgar, Campbell C. "On the Dating of the Fayum Portraits." *Journal of Hellenic Studies* 25 (1905): 225–33.

Ehrman, Bart D. *Forgery and Counterforgery: The Use of Literary Deceit in Early Christian Polemics.* Oxford University Press, 2012.

Elm, Susanna. "The Human Condition: *Condicio* and *Origo* in Augustine (Letters 10*, 20*, and 24*)." In *Making Sense of the Oath*, edited by Stephan Esders. Cultural Encounters. Brepols, forthcoming.

Elm, Susanna. "Inscriptions and Conversions: Gregory of Nazianzus on Baptism (*Or.* 38–40)." In *Conversion in Late Antiquity and the Middle Ages: Seeing and Believing*, edited by Kenneth Mills and Anthony Grafton. University of Rochester Press, 2003.

Elm, Susanna. "A Programmatic Life: Gregory of Nazianzus' *Orations* 42 and 43 and the Constantinopolitan Elites." *Arethusa* 33, no. 3 (2000): 411–27.

Elm, Susanna. *Sold: Augustine of Hippo on Slavery, Taxation, and Original Sin.* Manuscript in preparation.

Elm, Susanna. "Sold to Sin through *Origo*: Augustine of Hippo on Slavery and Freedom." *Studia Patristica* 98 (2017): 1–21.

Elm, Susanna. *Sons of Hellenism, Fathers of the Church: Emperor Julian, Gregory of Nazianzus, and the Vision of Rome.* Transformation of the Classical Heritage 49. University of California Press, 2012.

Elon, Amos. *Jerusalem: City of Mirrors.* Little, Brown, 1989.

Elsner, Jaś. "'Ancient Faces' at the British Museum." *Apollo* 146, no. 425 (July 1997): 48–49.

Fenton, James. "The Mummy's Secret." *New York Review of Books*, July 17, 1997.

Filer, Joyce M. "If the Face Fits . . . : A Comparison of Mummies and Their Accompanying Portraits Using Computerised Axial Tomography." In Bierbrier, *Portraits and Masks*.

Forbes-Robinson, John. *Illustrated London News*, June 30, 1888.

Frankfurter, David. *Christianizing Egypt: Syncretism and Local Worlds in Late Antiquity.* Princeton University Press, 2018.

Frankfurter, David. *Evil Incarnate: Rumors of Demonic Conspiracy and Satanic Abuse in History.* Princeton University Press, 2006.

Gilliam, Paul R. *Ignatius of Antioch and the Arian Controversy.* Brill, 2017.

Godfraind-De Becker, Anne. "Utilisations des momies de l'antiquité à l'aube du XXe siècle." *Revue des questions scientifiques* 181, no. 3 (2010): 306–40.

Goldhill, Simon. *Foucault's Virginity: Ancient Erotic Fiction and the History of Sexuality.* Cambridge University Press, 1995.

Grafton, Anthony. *Forgers and Critics: Creativity and Duplicity in Western Scholarship.* Princeton University Press, 1990.

Grant, Suzanna M. "Two 'Fayum' Portraits." *Bulletin of the Art Institute of Chicago* 72, no. 6 (November–December 1978): 2–4.

Graumann, Thomas. *The Acts of the Early Church Councils: Production and Character.* Oxford Early Christian Studies. Oxford University Press, 2021.

Graumann, Thomas. *Die Kirche der Väter: Vätertheologie und Väterbeweis in den Kirchen des Ostens bis zum Konzil von Ephesus (431).* Beiträge zur historischen Theologie 118. Mohr Siebeck, 2002.

Graumann, Thomas. "Orthodoxy, Authority, and Reconstruction of the Past in Church Councils." In *Invention, Rewriting, Usurpation: Discursive Fights over Religious Traditions in Antiquity*, edited by Jörg Ulrich, Anders-Christian Jacobsen, and David Brakke. Early Christianity in the Context of Antiquity 11. Peter Lang, 2011.

Gray, Patrick T. R. *Claiming the Mantle of Cyril: Cyril of Alexandria and the Road to Chalcedon.* Peeters, 2021.

Gray, Patrick T. R. "Covering the Nakedness of Noah: Reconstruction and Denial in the Age of Justinian." *Byzantinische Forschung* 24 (1997): 193–206.

Gray, Patrick T. R. "Forgery as an Instrument of Progress: Reconstructing the Theological Tradition in the Sixth Century." *Byzantinische Zeitschrift* 81, no. 2 (1988): 284–89.

Gray, Patrick T. R. "Neo-Chalcedonianism and the Tradition: From Patristic to Byzantine Theology." *Byzantinische Forschungen* 8 (1982): 61–70.

Gray, Patrick T. R. "'The Select Fathers': Canonizing the Patristic Past." *Studia Patristica* 23 (1989): 21–36.

Gschwantler, Kurt. "Graeco-Roman Portraiture." In Walker, *Ancient Faces*.

Guignebert, Charles. "Les demi-chrétiens et leur place dans l'église antique." *Revue de l'histoire des religions* 88 (1923): 65–102.

Guthrie, Steward. *Faces in the Clouds: A New Theory of Religion*. Oxford University Press, 1995.

Hainthaler, Theresia. "Die apollinaristischen Fälschungen und die christologischen Debatten des 5. und 6. Jahrhunderts: Einige Beobachtungen." In *Apollinarius und seine Folgen*, edited by Silke-Petra Bergjan, Bejamin Gleede, and Martin Heimgartner. Studien und Texte zu Antike und Christentum 93. Mohr Siebeck, 2015.

Hartman, Saidiya V. *Scenes of Subjection: Terror, Slavery, and Self-Making in Nineteenth-Century America*. Race and American Culture. Oxford University Press, 1997.

Henning, Meghan R. *Hell Hath No Fury: Gender, Disability, and the Invention of Damned Bodies in Early Christian Literature*. Yale University Press, 2021.

Hillner, Julia. "Empresses, Queens, and Letters: Finding a 'Female Voice' in Late Antiquity?" *Gender & History* 31, no. 2 (2019): 353–82.

Humfress, Caroline. "Law in Practice." In *A Companion to Late Antiquity*, edited by Philip Rousseau. Blackwell, 2009.

Jacobs, Andrew S. "'Ad religionis lucem de tenebris superstitionis': Jewish Converts under Christian Law." Paper given at the North American Patristics Society annual meeting, 2018.

Jacobs, Andrew S. "'Coloured by the Nature of Christianity': Nock's Invention of Religion and Ex-Jews in Late Antiquity." In *Celebrating Arthur Darby Nock: Choice, Change, and Conversion*, edited by Robert Matthew Calhoun, James A. Kelhoffer, and Clare R. Rothschild. Mohr Siebeck, 2021.

Jacobs, Andrew S. *Gospel Thrillers: Conspiracy, Fiction, and the Vulnerable Bible*. Cambridge University Press, 2023.

Jacobs, Andrew S. "'Solomon's Salacious Song': Foucault's Author Function and the Early Christian Interpretation of the *Canticum Canticorum*." *Medieval Encounters* 4, no. 1 (1998): 1–23.

Kleinkopf, Kathryn. "A Second Skin: Ascetics as Body-Places in Late Antique Christianity." PhD diss., University of Tennessee, 2019.

König, Jason, and Tim Whitmarsh. *Ordering Knowledge in the Roman Empire*. Cambridge University Press, 2007.

Kotrosits, Maia. *Rethinking Early Christian Identity: Affect, Violence, and Belonging*. Fortress, 2015.

Kotrosits, Maia, and Carly Daniel-Hughes. "Tertullian of Carthage and the Fantasy Life of Power: On Martyrs, Christians, and Other Attachments to Juridical Scenes." *Journal of Early Christian Studies* 28, no. 1 (2020): 1–31.

Kraemer, Ross Shepard. *Unreliable Witnesses: Religion, Gender, and History in the Greco-Roman Mediterranean*. Oxford University Press, 2012.

Kraus, Martin. "Rehearsing the Other Sex: Impersonation of Women in Ancient Classroom Ethopoeia." In *Escuela y Leteratura en Grecia*, edited by José Fernández Delgado, Francisca Pordomingo, and Antonio Stramaglia. Università degli Studi di Cassino, 2007.

Krawiec, Rebecca. *Shenoute and the Women of the White Monastery: Egyptian Monasticism in Late Antiquity*. Oxford University Press, 2002.

Lampe, G. W. H., and Henry George Liddell, eds. *A Patristic Greek Lexicon*. Clarendon, 1961.

Lehoux, Daryn. *What Did the Romans Know? An Inquiry into Science and Worldmaking*. University of Chicago Press, 2012.

Letteney, Mark, and Matthew D.C. Larsen. "A Roman Military Prison at Lambaesis." *Studies in Late Antiquity* 5, no. 1 (2021): 65–102.

Lietzmann, Hans. *Apollinaris von Laodicea und seine Schule: Texte und Untersuchungen*. Mohr Siebeck, 1904.

Liverani, Paolo. "I ritratti dipinto in età tardoantica." In *Figurationen des Porträts*, edited by Thierry Greub and Martin Roussel. Fink, 2018.

Löhr, Winrich A. "Religious Truth, Dissimulation, and Deception in Late Antique Christianity." In *Double Standards in the Ancient and Medieval World*, edited by Karla Pollman. Duehrkohp & Radicke, 2000.

Martínez, Javier. "Pseudepigraphy." In *A Companion to Late Antique Literature*, edited by Scott McGill and Edward J. Watts. Wiley, 2018.

McCloud, Scott. *Understanding Comics: The Invisible Art*. William Morrow, 1993.

Mena, Peter Anthony. *Place and Identity in the Lives of Antony, Paul, and Mary of Egypt: Desert as Borderland*. Religion and Spatial Studies. Palgrave MacMillan, 2019.

Metzger, Bruce. "Literary Forgeries and Canonical Pseudepigrapha." *Journal of Biblical Literature* 91, no. 1 (1972): 3–24.

Miller, Patricia Cox. "Is There a Harlot in This Text? Hagiography and the Grotesque." *Journal of Medieval and Early Modern Studies* 33, no. 3 (2003): 419–35.

Mills, Charles. *The Racial Contract*. Cornell University Press, 1997.

Miyazawa, Naomi. "Poe, the Portrait, and the Daguerreotype: Poe's Living Dead and the Visual Arts." *Poe Studies* 50 (2017): 88–106.

Montserrat, Dominic. "'To Make Death Beautiful': The Other Life of the Fayum Portraits." *Apollo* 150, no. 449 (July 1999), 18–25.

Moore, Alan. *Watchmen* #4, "Watchmaker." DC Comics, December 1986.

Moore, Christopher. *The Virtue of Agency: Sôphrosunê and Self-Constitution in Classical Greece*. Oxford University Press, 2023.

Moss, Yonatan. "'Packed with Patristic Testimonies': Severus of Antioch and the Reinvention of the Church Fathers." In *Between Personal and Institutional Religion: Self, Doctrine, and Practice in Late Antique Eastern Christianity*, edited by Brouria Bitton-Ashkelony and Lorenzo Perrone. Cultural Encounters in Late Antiquity and the Middle Ages 15. Brepols, 2013.

Muehlberger, Ellen. "The Legend of Arius's Death: Imagination, Space, and Filth in Late Ancient Historiography." *Past & Present* 227 (2015): 3–29.

Muehlberger, Ellen. *Moment of Reckoning: Imagined Death and Its Consequences in Late Ancient Christianity*. Oxford University Press, 2019.

Muehlberger, Ellen. "Perpetual Adjustment: The *Passion of Perpetua and Felicity* and the Entailments of Authenticity." *Journal of Early Christian Studies* 30, no. 3 (2022): 313–42.

Norri, Juhani. *Dictionary of Medical Vocabulary in English, 1375–1550: Body Parts, Sicknesses, Instruments, and Medical Preparations*. Routledge, 2016.

Nowicka, Maria. *Le portrait dans la peinture antique*. Academia Scientiarum Polona, 1993.

O'Connell, Elisabeth R. "Fayyum Portraits." In *Oxford Dictionary of Late Antiquity*, edited by Oliver Nicholson. Oxford University Press, 2018.

Pagello, Federico. "The 'Origin Story' is the Only Story: Seriality and Temporality in Superhero Fiction from Comics to Post-Television." *Quarterly Review of Film and Video* 34, no. 8 (2017): 725–45.

Parks, Sara, Shayna Sheinfeld, and Meredith J. C. Warren. *Jewish and Christian Women in the Ancient Mediterranean*. Routledge, 2021.

Parlasca, Klaus. "Introduzione." In Ricci, *el-Fayyum*.

Parlasca, Klaus. *Mumienporträts und verwandte Denkmaler*. Steiner, 1966.

Peirano, Irene. *Rhetoric of the Roman Fake: Latin Pseudepigrapha in Context*. Oxford University Press, 2012.

Perkinson, Stephen. *The Likeness of the King: A Prehistory of Portraiture in Late Medieval France*. University of Chicago Press, 2009.

Perrin, Michel-Yves. "*Crevit hypocrisis*: Limites d'adhésion au christianisme dans l'antiquité tardive; Entre histoire et historiographie." In *Le problème de la christianisation du monde antique*, edited by Hervé Inglebert, Sylvain Destephen, and Bruno Dumézil. Picard, 2010.

Petrie, W. M. Flinders. "The Earliest Racial Portraits." *Nature*, December 6, 1888, 128–30.

Price, Richard. "Conciliar Theology: Resources and Limitations." In *Die Synoden im trinitarischen Streit: Über die Etablierung eines synodalen Verfahrens und die Probleme seiner Anwendung im 4. und 5. Jahrhundert*, edited by Uta Heil and Annette von Stockhausen. Texte und Untersuchungen 177. De Gruyter, 2017.

Price, Richard. "The Second Council of Constantinople and the Malleable Past." In *Chalcedon in Context: Church Councils 400–700*, edited by Richard Price and Mary Whitby. Translated Texts for Historians, Contexts 1. Liverpool University Press, 2009.

Pylvänäinen, Pauliina. *Agents in Liturgy, Charity and Communication: The Tasks of Female Deacons in the Apostolic Constitutions*. Studia Traditionis Theologiae 37. Brepols, 2020.

Ray, John. "On the Way to Osiris." *Times Literary Supplement*, September 27, 1996, 36.

Rebillard, Éric. "A New Style of Argument in Christian Polemic: Augustine and the Use of Patristic Citations." *Journal of Early Christian Studies* 8, no. 4 (2000): 559–78.

Rebillard, Éric, and Jörg Rüpke, eds. *Group Identity and Religion Identity in Late Antiquity*. Catholic University of America Press, 2015.

Reed, Annette Yoshiko. "Method, Ethics, and Historiography: Tracing a Global Late Antiquity From and Beyond Christianity." *Ancient Jew Review*, January 26, 2022.

Ricci, Franco Maria. *el-Fayyum, introduzione e schede di Klaus Parlasca, testi di Jacques-Edouard Berger, Rosario Pintaud*. I segni dell'uomo 35. Franco Maria Ricci, 1985.

Rice, Yael, and Sonja Drimmer. "How Scientists Use and Abuse Portraiture." *Hyperallergic*, December 11, 2020.

Richlin, Amy. *Arguments with Silence: Writing the History of Roman Women*. University of Michigan Press, 2014.

Richter, F. H., Otto Donner von Richter, and Fritz von Ostini. *Katalog zu Theodor Grafs Gallerie antiker Porträts aus hellenistischer Zeit*. Berlin, 1889.

Riggs, Christina. *The Beautiful Burial in Roman Egypt: Art, Identity, and Funerary Religion*. Oxford University Press, 2006.

Roberts, Paul C. "'One of Our Mummies Is Missing': Evaluating Petrie's Records from Hawara." In Bierbrier, *Portraits and Masks*.

Rondot, Vincent. *Derniers visages des dieux d'Egypte: Iconographies, pantheons et cults dans le Fayoum hellénisé des IIe–IIIe siècles de notre ère*. Louvre, 2013.

Ronis, Sara. "It's a Roman . . . It's a Persian . . . It's Rabbi Meir! Secret Identities and the Rabbinic Self in the Babylonian Talmud." *Journal of Jewish Identities* 14, no. 1 (2021): 93–110.

Root, Marcus Aurelius. *The Camera and the Pencil, or the Heliographic Art*. Lippencott, 1864.

Roussell, Aline. *Porneia: On Desire and the Body in Antiquity*. Translated by Felicia Pheasant. Basil Blackwell, 1988.

Rüpke, Jörg. *On Roman Religion: Lived Religion and the Individual in Ancient Rome*. Cornell University Press, 2016.

Sargent, Anne Marie. "The Penitent Prostitute: The Tradition and Evolution of the 'Life of St. Mary the Egyptian.'" PhD diss., University of Michigan, 1977.

Scarry, Elaine. "The Difficulty of Imagining Other Persons." In *The Handbook of Interethnic Coexistence*, edited by Eugene Weiner. Continuum, 1998.

Schroeder, Caroline T. "Exemplary Women." In Chin and Schroeder, *Melania*.

Schroeder, Caroline T. *Monastic Bodies: Discipline and Salvation in Shenoute of Atripe*. University of Pennsylvania Press, 2007.

Sessa, Kristina. "Christianity and the Cubiculum: Spiritual Politics and Domestic Space in Late Antique Rome." *Journal of Early Christian Studies* 15, no. 2 (2007): 171–204.

Shepardson, Christine. "Posthumous Orthodoxy." In Chin and Schroeder, *Melania*.

Smith, Ali. *Artful*. Hamish Hamilton, 2012.

Smith, Shawn Michelle. *American Archives: Gender, Race, and Class in Visual Culture*. Princeton University Press, 1999.

Spiegelmann, Art. *Maus*. 2 vols. Pantheon, 1986 and 1991.

Spillers, Hortense J. "Mama's Baby, Papa's Maybe: An American Grammar Book." *Diacritics* 17, no. 2 (1987): 64–81.

Spinozzi, Adrienne. "Confronting, Collecting, and Celebrating Edgefield Stoneware." In *Hear Me Now: The Black Potters of Old Edgefield, South Carolina*, edited by Adrienne Spinozzi. Yale University Press, 2022.

Squatriti, Paolo. "Roofing Rome: Church Coverings and Power in the Postclassical City." In *Leadership and Community in Late Antiquity: Essays in Honour of Raymond Van Dam*, edited by Young Richard Kim and A. E. T. McLaughlin. Cultural Encounters in Late Antiquity and the Middle Ages 26. Brepols, 2020.

Stafford, Grace. "Between the Living and the Dead: Use, Reuse, and Imitation of Painted Portraits in Late Antiquity." *Journal of Roman Archaeology* 35, no. 2 (2022): 683–712.

Steedman, Carolyn Kay. "Mother Made Conscious: The Historical Development of a Primary School Pedagogy." *History Workshop Journal* 20 (1985): 149–63.

Stoker, Bram. *Famous Imposters*. Sturgis and Walton, 1910.
Stramaglia, Antonio. "Amori impossibili: P.Köln 250, le raccolte proginnasmatiche e la tradizione retorica dell' 'amante di un ritratto.'" In *Studium Declamatorium: Untersuchungen zu Schulübungen und Prunkreden von der Antike bis zur Neuzeit*, edited by Bianca-Jeanette Schröder and Jens-Peter Schröder. Beiträge zur Altertumskunde 176. Sauer, 2003.
Taylor, John. "Before the Portraits: Burial Practices in Pharaonic Egypt." In Walker, *Ancient Faces*.
Thistlewood, Jean, Olivia Dill, Marc S. Walker, and Andrew Shortland. "Study of the Relative Locations of Facial Features within Mummy Portraits." In *Mummy Portraits of Roman Egypt: Emerging Research from the APPEAR Project*, edited by Marie Svoboda and Caroline R. Cartwright. Getty Museum, 2010.
Thomassen, Einar. Review of *Forgery and Counterforgery: The Use of Literary Deceit in Early Christian Polemics*, by Bart D. Ehrman. *Journal of Theological Studies*, n.s., 65 (2014): 243.
Thompson, D. L. "A Patchwork Fayum in Toledo." *American Journal of Archaeology* 77, no. 4 (1973): 438–39.
Tuilier, André. "Remarques sur les frauds des Apollinaristes et des Monophysites: Notes de critique textuelle." In *Texte und Textkritik: Eine Aufsatzsammlung*, edited by Jürgen Dummer. Akademie Verlag, 1987.
Vessey, Mark. "The Forging of Orthodoxy in Latin Christian Literature: A Case Study." *Journal of Early Christian Studies* 4, no. 4 (1996): 495–513.
Virchow, R. L. C. *Portrait-Muenzen und Graf's hellenistische Portrait-Galerie*. Berlin, 1902.
Walker, Susan, ed. *Ancient Faces: Mummy Portraits from Roman Egypt*. Routledge, 1997.
Walker, Susan. "Mummy Portraits and Roman Portraiture." In Walker, *Ancient Faces*.
Ward, Benedicta. *Harlots of the Desert: A Study of Repentance in Early Monastic Sources*. Cistercian, 1987.
Weber, Graham. "Giving the Dead Their Due: An Exhibition Re-Examines Funerary Portraits from Roman Egypt." In *Funerary Portraits from*

Roman Egypt. https://harvardartmuseums.org/article/giving-the-dead-their-due-an-exhibition-re-examines-funerary-portraits-from-roman-egypt.

Weitzman, Steven P. *Surviving Sacrilege: Cultural Persistence in Jewish Antiquity*. Harvard University Press, 2005.

Wessel, Susan. "Literary Forgery and the Monothelete Controversy: Some Scrupulous Uses of Deception." *Greek, Roman, and Byzantine Studies* 42 (2001): 201–20.

Whelan, Robin. "Surrogate Fathers: Imaginary Dialogue and Patristic Culture in Late Antiquity." *Early Medieval Europe* 25, no. 1 (2017): 19–37.

Wilkinson, Kate. *Women and Modesty in Late Antiquity*. Cambridge University Press, 2015.

Williams, Linda. *Hard Core: Power, Pleasure, and the "Frenzy of the Visible."* University of California Press, 1989.

Woods, Marjorie Curry. *Weeping for Dido: The Classics in the Medieval Classroom*. Princeton University Press, 2019.

INDEX

abolitionists, white, 36–38
Abraham, 2
Acts of Paul and Thecla, 112
agency, in speeches in character, 22–27, 52
Anatolius (pagan), 80–81
Anonymous Sequel, 28–29; author of, 29, 34–35; judgment of others and stereotyping in, 31–34; and the *Life of Mary of Egypt*, 44–45; spiritual combat evoked in, 29–30
Apelles, 147
apocalyptic: meaning of, 6; Christian information gathering as, 85–86
Apollinarius of Laodicea, 101
Apollo, portrait of, 81
ascetics: dwellings of, 69–70; spiritual combat of, 30
Athanasius of Alexandria: and Apollinarius of Laodicea, 101; and Cyril of Alexandria, 96, 100–101; orthodox reputation of, 96–97; writings by and attributed to, 97–98
Augustine of Hippo: on Christianness, 53–54; *Confessions*, 53–54, 59–61; doubts about Christianness of, 59–61; on new Christians, 56–59, 65–66; pears stolen by, 33–34

baptism, motives for, 58–59
body: and buildings, 69–72, 76; of the superfather, 114–15
body-place, 69–70
Brown, Peter: *Power and Persuasion in Late Antiquity*, 47–48
buildings: ascetics' dwellings, 69–70; and doubts about Christianness, 55–56; and enforcement of orthodoxy, 66–69; people imbricated with, 69–70, 76; as proof of religious practice, 70–72. *See also* houses

Christ: Cyril of Alexandria on the nature of, 100; in the *Letter to the Hebrews*, 1, 3–4
Christianity: growth of, 6–7, 56; patterns of knowing in, 5–10
Christianness: and Augustine of Hippo, 53–54, 59–61; and duplexity of human beings, 65–66; marks of and doubts about, 55, 57–59, 61–62; and property, 55–56, 70
Church History (John of Ephesus), 79–83
classroom, rhetorical, 21
comic drawing, 154–55
Confessions (Augustine), 53–54, 59–61
Constantine, 68–69
converts: evaluation of, 61–62; motives of, 58–59
Copts, 136
Council of Chalcedon, 104
Council of Ephesus, 98
cubiculum, 70
Cyril of Alexandria, 98–99; on Athanasius, 96; Athanasius wrongly cited by, 100–103; on Christ's nature, 100; Ibas's letter about, 103–4; on posthumous condemnation, 116; as super-father, 10–11, 102, 115–16, 119; *Third Letter to Nestorius*, 99
Cyril of Scythopolis, 41

death, as evidence of evil, 85
demons: in the *Anonymous Sequel*, 30; in persons and houses, 74–76
disease: as evidence of evil, 85; in photography and Fayyum portraits, 139
divinity, late ancient knowledge of, 93–94
Douglass, Frederick, 134

Doxiadis, Euphrosyne: *The Mysterious Fayum Portraits*, 140, 148–49

Ecclesiastical History (Socrates), 58–59
ecumenical councils, 87–89. *See also names of individual councils*
education, rhetorical, 21. *See also speeches in character*
Egypt: European interest in products from, 130–31; and Fayyum portraits, 141–45
el-Fayyum, 139–40
empathy: and speeches in character, 35–36, 38; and ventriloquizing the other, 36–38
Epistle of Barnabas, 112
ethnography, ancient, 9
eunuch, speeches in character as, 16
Eusebius of Caesarea: on Constantine's ban on pagan worship, 68–69; on converts' motives, 59; on destruction of pagan buildings, 71–72; on fake Christians, 66; *Life of Constantine*, 59, 71–72

faith, in the *Letter to the Hebrews*, 1–2, 4–6
family albums, 138
fathers of the church, 95; anthologizing the works of, 97; attribution of works to, 97–98, 105; authority of, 98; and forgery, 105–6; as ontological phenomenon, 113–14. *See also names of individual fathers*
Fayyum portraits, 11, 120; artistic tradition thought to be evidenced by, 147–49; in coffee table books, 139–40; cultural origins assigned to, 141–46;

and disease, 139; and diversity, 150–51; and ethnicity and lineage, 140–41; excavators and dealers of, 127–29; at exhibitions, 124–25; ignored until nineteenth century, 129–30; individuality of subjects in, 133–35, 152–53; modern reactions to, 121–23, 140–41, 151–52; original functions and contexts of, 125–27; and photography, 123–24, 134–35, 137; production of, 127–29, 131–32, 155–56; and race science, 135–38; realism of, 154–55

Flinders Petrie, William Matthew: and mummy portraits, 129–31; and race science, 135–37

forgery: as deviance and deception, 108–9; and early Christian literature, 111–12; and intention, 109–11; in late ancient Christianity, 105–8, 112–13; letter of Ibas as, 104; and superfathers, 119

Galton, Francis, 137–38
Gayet, Albert-Jean, 129
Gesios, Shenoute's campaign against, 72–78
Girl with a Pearl Earring (Vermeer), 153
God Is Blessed (Shenoute), 76
Gospels, 111–12
Graf, Theodor, 127–28
Great Lakes, 63

Heliopolis, heathens at, 79–81
heresiology, 9
heresy, 66–68
holy man, spiritual combat of, 30
houses: and demons, 75–76; of Heliopolitan heathens, 79–81; and knowledge about individuals, 10, 55–56, 70–71, 76–78, 83; people imbricated with, 69–71, 76; religious activity in, 70–71; Shenoute breaks into, 73–78

human being: demons residing in, 74–75; duplex nature of, 65–66; as object to be known, 8–9; pagan buildings envisioned as, 71–72; property imbricated with, 69–71, 76

Ibas of Edessa, letter on Cyril of Alexandria by, 103–4
ignorance: general shape of, 62–64, 66; and speeches in character, 51–52
impossible woman, 20, 25–28; Mary of Egypt as, 45–47; pleasure in creation of, 52
Interdepartmental Program in Ancient History (University of Michigan), 150

Jesus. *See* Christ
John of Ephesus: *Church History*, 79–83
Josephus, 64
Justinian: *On the Orthodox Faith*, 104n25; and posthumous condemnation, 117–18

knowledge: and affect, 12; as analytical term, 7; Christian, 5–7; and Christian power, 85–86; of the divine, 93–94; of individuals via their houses, 10, 55–56, 70–71, 76–78, 83; late ancient creation and maintaining of, 7–10; and riddles, 152; and speeches in character, 20, 49–52; and tradition, 12–13. *See also* ignorance

Lake Erie, 63
Lake Superior, 63
lecture series, 11
Let Our Eyes (Shenoute), 74–75
Letter to the Hebrews, 1–6, 112
Libanius of Antioch, speech in character by, 22–28; and the *Life of Mary of Egypt*, 42
Life of Constantine (Eusebius), 59, 71–72
Life of Mary of Egypt: dating, authorship, and summary of, 40–41; and the impossible woman, 45–47; and the prostitute come to her senses, 42–43; repentance and transformation unrecognized in, 44–45; and trope of repentant woman in the wild, 41–42

Mary of Egypt. See *Life of Mary of Egypt*
masking, in illustration, 155
Melania the Younger, 47
monk, spiritual combat of, 30
Moschus, John: *Spiritual Meadow*, 41
Moses, 2
mumiya, 130
mummies: and Fayyum portraits, 126–27; products made from, 130
mummy brown, 130
mummy portraits. See Fayyum portraits
Mysterious Fayum Portraits, The (Doxiadis), 140

Natural History (Pliny), 146–47
Noah, 2, 107–8

observational selectivity, 49–50
On the Orthodox Faith (Justinian), 104n25

pagans: ban on worship of, 68–69; buildings of, 71–72
painting, 146–47. See also Fayyum portraits
Paul the Apostle, 33–34
Philo of Alexandria, 64
photography: and disease, 139; Fayyum portraits compared to, 123; and the individual, 132–35; and racial lineage, 137–38, 140
Placidia, heathens at, 82–83
Pliny the Elder: *Natural History*, 146–47
Pontianus, 117
pornē, 17–18. See also prostitute come to her senses, figure of
portraiture: and Fayyum portraits, 122–24; in Greco-Roman painting, 146–47; and photography, 132–33
posthumous condemnation, 116–18
power, in late antiquity, 83–85
Power and Persuasion in Late Antiquity (Brown), 47–48
property. See buildings; houses
prostitute come to her senses, figure of: in the *Anonymous Sequel*, 29–34; in Libanius's model speech in character, 22–28; as persistent example and shared reference point, 49–52; speech in character prompt for, 15–18
pseudepigraphy, 109–10

race science, 135–38
Rankin, John, 37

realism, 153–55
religious deviance: invasiveness in search for, 82–83; and property, 66–68; violence in evaluation of, 86
Rembrandt, 153
riddles, 152
Rufinus (pagan), 79–80
Rufinus of Aquileia, 72

Second Council of Constantinople, 89; and Cyril of Alexandria, 11–12, 104; discounted and lamented, 89–91; and forgery, 106–7; and the superfather, 92–93, 119
Shenoute of Atripe: on demons within non-Christians, 74–75; and Gesios, 73, 75–78; *God Is Blessed*, 76; on houses of wicked people, 75–76; *Let Our Eyes*, 74–75; violence justified by, 73–74, 86
Simplicianus, 53–54
slaves, Black, 36–38
Socrates of Constantinople: *Ecclesiastical History*, 58–59
Sophronius of Jerusalem, 40
sōphrosynē, 17
speeches in character, 10, 14–16; boy composers of, 38, 47–48; and empathy, 35–38; as eunuch, 16; and knowledge, 20, 49–52; and mastery, 20, 38–39; pleasure in exercise of, 52; as prostitute, 15–18, 22–28; as women, 18–19
Spiritual Meadow (John Moschus), 41
students, rhetorical, 38, 47–48

superfather, 92–93, 102–3; body of, 114–15; Cyril of Alexandria as, 10–11, 102, 115–16; and forgery, 119; and time, 115–16

Temple in Jerusalem, 64
Tertullian, 84
Theodosian Code, 58, 82
Theodosius II, 116
Third Letter to Nestorius (Cyril of Alexandria), 99
tradition: and knowledge, 12–13; silent assimilation as respect for, 94
translation, 4
tronies, 153
Tsarouchis, Yannis, 149

University of Michigan, 150–51

Valle, Pietro delle, 129–30
ventriloquizing: in the *Life of Mary of Egypt*, 45–46; of the other, 36–38
Vermeer, Johannes: *Girl with a Pearl Earring*, 153
Victorinus, 53–54
violence: and religious deviance, 86; and Shenoute of Atripe, 73–74, 86

White Monastery, 76
women: and men's knowledge of them, 49–52; sources about, 48; in speeches in character, 18–19
writing, Christian: citational habits in, 94–95; and forgery, 105–13. *See also specific titles*

Zosimus, 40–41, 43–46

Founded in 1893,
UNIVERSITY OF CALIFORNIA PRESS
publishes bold, progressive books and journals
on topics in the arts, humanities, social sciences,
and natural sciences—with a focus on social
justice issues—that inspire thought and action
among readers worldwide.

The UC PRESS FOUNDATION
raises funds to uphold the press's vital role
as an independent, nonprofit publisher, and
receives philanthropic support from a wide
range of individuals and institutions—and from
committed readers like you. To learn more, visit
ucpress.edu/supportus.

www.ingramcontent.com/pod-product-compliance
Lightning Source LLC
Chambersburg PA
CBHW030654230426
43665CB00011B/1095